KICKING THE STARS

*Rediscovering Our Trust in God
in the Midst of Crisis*

Wendell E. Hutchins II

WESTBOW
PRESS®
A DIVISION OF THOMAS NELSON
& ZONDERVAN

This book is a work of non-fiction. Unless otherwise noted, the author and the publisher make no explicit guarantees as to the accuracy of the information contained in this book and in some cases, names of people and places have been altered to protect their privacy.

WestBow Press books may be ordered through booksellers or by contacting:

WestBow Press
A Division of Thomas Nelson & Zondervan
1663 Liberty Drive
Bloomington, IN 47403
www.westbowpress.com
844-714-3454

Because of the dynamic nature of the Internet, any web addresses or links contained in this book may have changed since publication and may no longer be valid. The views expressed in this work are solely those of the author and do not necessarily reflect the views of the publisher, and the publisher hereby disclaims any responsibility for them.

Any people depicted in stock imagery provided by Getty Images are models, and such images are being used for illustrative purposes only. Certain stock imagery © Getty Images.

Unless marked otherwise, all Scripture quotations are taken from the King James Version.

Scripture quotations marked NIV are taken from The Holy Bible, New International Version®, NIV® Copyright © 1973, 1978, 1984, 2011 by Biblica, Inc.® Used by permission. All rights reserved worldwide.

Scripture quotations marked MSG are taken from The Message. Copyright © 1993, 1994, 1995, 1996, 2000, 2001, 2002. Used by permission of NavPress Publishing Group.

Scripture quotations marked ESV taken from The Holy Bible, English Standard Version® (ESV®), Copyright © 2001 by Crossway, a publishing ministry of Good News Publishers. All rights reserved.

Scripture quotations marked AMP are taken from the Amplified® Bible, Copyright © 2015 by The Lockman Foundation. Used by permission.

Scripture quotations marked TPT are from The Passion Translation®. Copyright © 2017, 2018 by Passion & Fire Ministries, Inc. Used by permission. All rights reserved. ThePassionTranslation.com.

ISBN: 978-1-6642-5609-5 (sc)
ISBN: 978-1-6642-5610-1 (hc)
ISBN: 978-1-6642-5611-8 (e)

Library of Congress Control Number: 2022901481

Print information available on the last page.

WestBow Press rev. date: 02/17/2022

This book is dedicated to Rev. Dr. C. L. Dees and Bishop C. G. "Jabo" Green with great gratitude for their lives and ministries.

Dr. Dees was my childhood pastor. He was renowned for his revelatory teaching and his brilliant, expository preaching.

Pastor Dees taught me about the value and merits of theology in both principle and practice. He taught me the importance of pursuing a mastery of language so that we might better articulate the Word of God to others. He believed that one who "studies to show himself/herself approved of God" should include the discipline of creating an ever-expanding lexicon. He instilled in me the belief that to "preach and teach the Word of God" is the greatest privilege and highest calling for any person. As was his aim, so is mine: to prayerfully stir your heart, renew your passion, and/or perhaps create a new level of hunger and love for the Holy Scriptures.

Dr. Dees inspired me to always be a student with an insatiable desire for learning, a seeker of wisdom, and a pursuer of God filled with His knowledge. Pastor Dees introduced me to a missional mindset, teaching me to love the people of the world, from every continent, from every plain, from every shore.

Before permitting us the opportunity to travel on a mission overseas, he "proved" our desire for ministry in the local church and throughout our city. In order to be qualified for a trip overseas, we were expected to be accomplished "missionaries" (I use the term loosely) to our own schools, marketplaces, and neighborhoods.

Dr. Dees was a well-respected professor and guest lecturer at seminaries and universities around the world. His lectures frequently included subjects such as: The Love of God through Christ; Justification by Faith; The Covenant of Abraham; The Gospel of Love; Jesus, the Christ; The One Lord; The Landlord; The Doctrine of Water and Spirit; New Creation Man, The New Creation Mind, and many more. One of the great privileges of my life was having Brother and Sister Dees join us after his retirement from his beloved church. Ann and I, along with our entire Church of Champions, loved serving him until his death in 2005. To this day, we cherish him and continue to honor him by maintaining his personal office and a portion of his library. Again, words are not adequate to express my love for Pastor and Lady Dees.

In 1982, my wife and I relocated and joined the vibrant community of faith led by Pastor C. G. "Jabo" Green in Spring, Texas. Spring Tabernacle was an incredible oasis of love and grace to us, a place that allowed us to relax and heal. Bishop Green has served as my pastor from 1982 to the present. I cannot begin to tell you how much I love Bishop and First Lady Green. Pastor Green healed me. He restored my confidence. He showed me what the grace of God looks like in Wrangler jeans. He taught me that compassion for people and the love of God often wear the same Ropers. Pastor Green showed me that our theology "about" God's love is of little value to people if it cannot work in the environs of their daily challenges, struggles, disappointments, brokenness, and pain.

Bishop Green formed my future out of the pains of my past by openly challenging me to do what I had said I would not do. He appointed me to the ministry when I was determined to sit on the sidelines. He sent me out knowing that I had premeditatedly determined that I would hide within. He blessed me when I didn't deserve one ounce of it, and he continued loving me when I was unlovable. Whatever I have become for God, and whatever achievements I might enjoy today, are all a credit to His love for me, and all honor goes to God and Pastor C. G. "Jabo" Green.

Bishop Green is fearless. He was the one man in my youth who could not be intimidated. He is not a man of partiality, regardless of one's last name. Neither is he influenced in his convictions about people. For he is a lover of people, and, as a result, he sees the value, the good, the purpose, and the call in each of his people's lives. He refused to allow me to settle for sitting in the bleachers of ministry. He was having none of it. He wanted my best effort then, and he expects to see my best work now.

If you know Bishop Green, you'll know that he does not take no for an answer. He never quits on a project. He never stops until he completes his task or achieves his goal. He sets out to win the prize and rarely, if ever, fails to do so. He is a man of sterling character, and his word is his bond.

I give thanks to God every day that Pastor Green took me in as his own spiritual son, making me one of his very own boys. He has never stopped loving me, and as a result, I remain extraordinarily blessed because he has been my steady head, my covering, and my government. He taught me the value of grace with a weed eater and ministry with a bale of hay. I am so grateful for his and Sister Green's immeasurable love for me and our family. With his fatherly love, his unique patience, and the First Lady's famous chocolate pie, I am kicking the stars.

Pastor Dees taught me the laws and science necessary to reach the dizzying heights of wondrous revelation, that astonishing region where luminary marvel burns bright. Pastor Green taught me how to soar into the stratosphere of faith, believing that God's best for me was united to me by my obedience and faithfulness to His Word.

To possess a theology with a cosmic view, or to boast of an expertise in the laws and science of the Spirit is for some people abstract philosophy. I have found that often, pseudo-philosophers are those people who've been to the water's edge in their Red Sea moment, but rather than stretching their faith to see what would happen, or if the "impossible" would be rolled back, they stepped back and huddled—they huddled long enough to give birth to a litany of "what-ifs" and "what could be's." Instead of launching into the adventure before them, or shooting for the stars, they chose to construct a laboratory out of their thoughts and ideas, becoming self-made experts who will never "see" what they readily propose or live in the reality of what they "think."

What people are saying about...

KICKING THE STARS

During a tumultuous transition period of my life, God led me to Dr. Wendell Hutchins. I arrived at a gathering Dr. Hutchins was hosting as a stranger, but I left with a friend and brother who has been a perpetual blessing to my life and ministry ever since. I arrived with questions but left with wisdom. Countless lives can testify to the same experience with Dr. Hutchins and his gift for finding solutions, strategies, and healing.

Through *Kicking the Stars*, you'll read the Rhema Word of God, crafted and articulated as only Dr. Hutchins can, so that you clearly understand what "sayeth the Lord."

— Tony Suarez, Revivalmakers, www.tonysuarez.com

Wendell is a guy who has demonstrated during decades of ministry that he lives out the things he writes about. He is a pastor and friend to me, so I am always paying attention to what he has to say and write.

— Greg Gibbs, author and lead navigator at Auxano

Kicking the Stars is a guidepost to the church in this post-pandemic world. Bishop Wendell Hutchins brings profound thinking and solutions to a subject that is on the minds of us all. A man of integrity and wisdom, Bishop Hutchins speaks truth in an age of confusion and fear. When you read it, you'll discover God taking you into the future He has designed for you.

—Nathaniel Nix, senior pastor, Pineview Church

In his first letter to the Corinthian church, the apostle Paul wrote, "If the trumpet does not sound a clear call, who will get ready for battle?" Paul chose to illustrate his words using the trumpet because its clear, brilliant tone can be heard above the din of battle. Wendell Hutchins likewise trumpets a clear and decisive sound in *Kicking the Stars*. The words on these pages confidently call the reader into the winnable battle for hope, both personally and corporately. Scriptural accuracy blows the fog away and reveals reasons we can be positive about today and tomorrow. Wendell Hutchins has again pinpointed the solution available to us all.

—Brett Jones, senior pastor, Grace Church Humble

I have known Pastor Hutchins for several years, and since the very moment I met him, he has made a lasting impact on my life, family, and ministry. This is why I am not surprised at how amazingly impactful his book, *Kicking the Stars,* is! This book is written from the mind and spirit of one of God's generals of the faith—and he has paved the way for many, including me!

—Randy Coggins II, senior pastor, Echo Church

A long stride for a merry ride. Life is full of sudden happenings that must be dealt with unplanned reactions. The virus stopped us in our tracks—not just us but the world. Come on, smart man, awaken the greatness in us, revive us, inspire us, and kick us! Spent our life with numbers, and suddenly we had only ten. Not just us, everybody had only ten! Where comes the inspiration for a locked-down generation? Solomon said under the sun! But failure was constant, so it must be above the sun! That weary pilgrim is where the stars dwell! We must kick-start the stars. Stardust is the answer to bring glitter to a dull existence. Only Wendell Hutchins has the long stride and unlimited expression to reach above the sun and kick-start the stars.

— Kenneth Phillips, Bishop, Promiseland Church

Dr. Wendell Hutchins, in this his latest work, takes us all aboard a fishing boat named *Discouragement*, at once daring disciples try to reset after suffering debilitating defeat. Their dilemma: they had more questions than caught fish. Then, only to see Jesus standing on the sandy shores of the sea called Galilee. Cooking up something called hope! The aroma of an answer was so appealing, one named Peter did not think to take off his coat before diving in. Not a good swimming strategy. I use this analogy to "amen" Dr. Hutchins emphatically stating that the Word of God (our garment, our coat) is the absolute answer to life's questions. The Word of God may seem "all wet" to some and "too heavy" to others, but the struggle to hope's shore secures the answers that makes apostles out of anglers! *Kicking the Stars* will repay you many times over as our author reminds us that the brightest stars come out on the darkest nights. We all thank you, sir, for taking on this herculean task as only you could have. We are eternally grateful for your voice of encouragement to the body of Christ around the world!

— Dr. Louis Green, chancellor, GPS Seminary; bishop, ACTS
   Christian Network

Wendell Hutchins is a rare vessel of honor. His unique style of writing and speaking puts him in a league of his own. Compile that with effective ministry of seeing lives transformed from the most extreme circumstances over several decades, and you have his pedigree. If you are feeling discouraged or hopeless, this book is for you. If you are not sure your life can matter, this book is for you. If anyone has ever told you that your mistakes have ended your spiritual walk, this book is for you. As the song says, "If I'm not dead, He's not done." In these pages, you will find more than words. You will discover people and their stories. They will challenge you, encourage you, and make you laugh with joy in celebration of their victories while believing anew for your own.

— Anthony Langston, senior pastor, Tapestry Church

I can honestly say that Pastor W. E. Hutchins is the single greatest influence of my life. He has been a pastor, mentor, father, and friend. His teachings and words of wisdom over the past twenty years have helped shape my life as well as my understanding of who God is. He has shown me how much I am loved, and he's taught me how to discover God's plan for my life. I cannot wait to put my hands on every piece of material he produces. He is a wordsmith for the ages, and God blesses everything he puts his hand to—and everything he writes is full of revelation. If you want your life changed for the better, read this book!

—James Wyatt, three-time American Ninja Warrior finalist, Elite Obstacle Course champion, and owner of BC Fitness

During times of intense trial, struggle, and loss, the words of Bishop Hutchins have encouraged me, taught me, strengthened me, and given me incredible hope in the power and grace of God. He has shown me that through times of failure, transition, and even my own weaknesses, God's strength is made perfect.

Kicking the Stars is a riveting book that builds your faith and causes you to know that you can rise from the dust of adverse circumstances to behold the glorious purpose of God for your life.

If you are ready to exchange the charred ashes of your life for the beauty that God has designed for you, I encourage you to get this book. It will change your life!

—Rashall Hightower, senior pastor, Living Word Worship Center

I recognized his name, Bishop Wendell Hutchins. I had heard it before. After feeling compelled within, I moved to Houston. I rented a place from a friend of a friend. She said, "If you need a good church to go to, try Church of Champions. Wendell Hutchins is the pastor. He's my favorite preacher. He is an eloquent speaker."

I had just held a worship conference at my friend's great church outside of Detroit. He said, "My father in the faith is Bishop Wendell

Hutchins in Houston. He's *my* bishop and *my* pastor." I knew I had to meet this man.

I reached out to Bishop Hutchins, and I soon realized why I moved to Houston. I survived because of the anointing on Bishop Hutchins's ministry. Others will survive because of this man's mighty ministry. For fourteen months, I moved my ministry office and my home to Houston. I now know the reason for this important season was to know my friend Bishop Hutchins and to attend a weekend encounter with God, Emmaus, and Beyond, a God-breathed ministry vision from the heart of Wendell Hutchins.

I just finished reading the Spirit-drenched words of life contained within Wendell Hutchins brand-new book, *Kicking the Stars*. Because of Bishop Hutchins's anointed quill, someone will survive today.

— Jeff Ferguson, Grammy-, Stellar-, and Dove-Award-Winning songwriter and gospel minister

We are living in a day where the voice of a father is so needed. In this book, you will hear the voice of a father speaking to generations before us and generations to come.

—Bishop Tony Hall

In this hour, there are but a few ministries of the Gospel that actually preach and teach from intensive Bible study and the study of original languages. The world is rife with internet sermons, canned theological teachings, and ghostwritten stories.

Not so with Dr. Wendell Hutchins. He is the genuine article amid the many who are wannabes. Each word you read in *Kicking the Stars* comes forth from the Word of God, and it has been given to him under the influence of the Holy Ghost. It is as the Bible says. Dr. Hutchins is a man who God has moved beyond merely knowing the "acts of God" to a prophet who knows "the ways of our God" (Psalm 103:7).

The one regret that may come out of reading this revelatory

book is that you have not had the opportunity to meet Dr. Hutchins. Enjoy the revelations that await you. And, by all means, find a way to hear this man of God preach and meet him personally. Be blessed by the book, and once again, let me encourage you to press to hear him as well as meet him. I highly recommend the reading of this book and getting to know the man of God, Wendell Hutchins.

—Dr. John F. Avanzini

CONTENTS

Foreword

Abram was in a dilemma. He had received a promise from God Almighty regarding his family, but he was childless. He needed a son who would be his descendant and heir. In Abram's thinking, one would be enough.

Genesis 15:5 in the Living Bible says, "Then God brought Abram outside beneath the nighttime sky and told him, 'Look up into the heavens and count the stars if you can. Your descendants will be like that—too many to count!'"

God didn't want to give Abram only one son. He wanted to give him many sons—too many to count. God gave Abram a change of perspective. He needed to be able to see things from God's point of view instead of from his own circumstances. God brought Abram out from his tent and told him to look up. As he did, he didn't just see the same stars he had seen many times before. He began to see his future the way God saw it—and the future was limitless.

We need more visionaries who are not afraid to go beyond man-made limitations and natural circumstances. We need men like Dr. Wendell Hutchins who dare to dream—and who are not afraid to boldly declare their dreams to a skeptical and even hostile culture. Even more importantly, Dr. Hutchins is one of those rare people who have the courage, the determination, and the willingness to work relentlessly to see their dream become reality.

Dr. Hutchins had a dream more than a quarter century ago

that has developed into a worldwide ministry that fuses academic understanding with supernatural distinctive. As a result, he has a profound and abiding influence on leaders, churches, and communities. It has been a pleasure and a privilege to celebrate him joining forces with us here at the City Harvest Network to reach even more multitudes for the kingdom of God.

In *Kicking the Stars*, Dr. Hutchins encourages you to get outside the tent of your constraints and look up. As you do, the limitations of this world's system will lose their hold on you. The restraints that others have used to confine you will fall away. The apprehensions and misgivings of a culture that has turned away from God will no longer bind you.

Looking down is fine when using the stairs. Looking around is necessary when crossing the street. But *Kicking the Stars* will inspire you to look up so that you can expand your horizons, obtain your dreams, and achieve your true God-given purpose.

—Dr. Rod Parsley, pastor and founder, World Harvest Church, Columbus, Ohio

Introduction

In *Garden, Park, Glen, Meadow*, Leonard Sweet wrote, "There is an old Latin expression: *tempora mutantur et nos, mutamur in illis*— 'times change and we change with them.' In times of change, the Christian does not go back to zero, but to origin. When it comes to Christ and culture, we do not start over from scratch, but we start from our origins. True originality is a homecoming; not an overturning of doctrines but a return to the origins of the faith."

Once delivered to the saints! Sweet was right to say, "We do not go back to zero, we go back to our origin." Today, while our culture is reeling from the throes and aftermath of a worldwide pandemic, the good news is that the church of Jesus Christ is rising in her victorious power and preaching the redemptive message that is made alive by the power and witness of its origins.

Kicking the Stars is a collaboration of stories born out of life lessons and experiences that prove that the principles and practices of the inspired, inerrant, infallible, and irrevocable Word of God is the absolute truth that is designed to work through our lives into and through our culture. Thus, our doctrinal origin is divinely designed to inform our modern societal landscape and not vice versa.

Like Paul, with his encouraging helper Barnabas, who left Jerusalem to reach the pagan worshippers of Aphrodite in Corinth, this book is written with a prayer that you will be inspired to share the Gospel of Jesus with a renewed passion for those who are lost and hurting, as well as to encourage you with life lessons learned while navigating a post-Christian landscape with the help of the truths gathered from the origins of the Christian faith:

> When the Church is absolutely different from the world, she invariably attracts it. It is then that the world is made to listen to her message, though it may hate it at the first. (D. Martyn Lloyd-Jones)

> While we weren't paying attention, everything changed—our world eroded from a Christian era to a post-Christian era. It's a new kind of Dark Ages! (Charles R. Swindoll)

> What the Church needs today is not more or better machinery, not new organizations, or more novel methods. The Church needs men and women whom the Holy Spirit can use—men and women of prayer, men and women mighty in prayer. The Holy Spirit does not flow through methods, but through men … He does not anoint plans, but men and women of prayer! (E. M. Bounds)

> The grass withers, the flower fades, but the Word of God stands forever. (Isaiah 40:8)

1

Did You Know about This Highway?

Too often, we allow the perimeter of the possibilities in our lives to shrink to the area that we can "see." We forfeit the grand scale of our universe of opportunities when we become parochial in our views and only see things through the lenses of our immediate circumstances and needs.

Are you aware that you can access the longest drivable road in the world here in the United States?

The Pan-American Highway passes through fourteen countries and is 48,000 kilometers—or 29,825 miles—long. Don't let small-minded thinkers influence your future and turn you away from the magnitude of your promise and possibilities. Don't allow "wrong-thinking" people in your circle of influence to convince you that the world is a disconnected place where intelligent people should isolate themselves from the conspiracies being peddled by the merchants of fear.

These people are infected with the paralysis of their analysis! They validate their beliefs about life and their perceptions of the future by their ability to convince you that their point of view is the only valid one. They spend their time and energy convincing you that unless you are afraid of their fears, your view of life is pedestrian at best—and more likely completely wrong.

Don't ever forget you are God's masterpiece of creation. It is through God's very own workmanship that He uses you as a partner in His divine plan of redemption. God made you to "have dominion over the works of your hands; He has put all things under your feet" (Psalm 8:6).

Dream big. Be confident. Live bold. Go ... kicking the stars!

As certainly as people can travel through a "hemisphere of difference and diversity," humanity was made to discover heavenly realities. We are reminded that there is only one highway that leads to the victory that comes from above. For Jesus said, "I Am the Way ... no man cometh unto the Father except through Me" (John 14:6).

> A highway will be there, a roadway, and it shall be called the Highway of Holiness. The unclean will not travel on it, but it will be for him who walks that way. And fools will not wander on it. No lion will be there, nor will any vicious beast go up on it ... but the redeemed will walk there. (Isaiah 35:8–10)

Our spiritual and mental disposition in a time of crisis is a marker of our maturity. Crisis reveals the evidence of our experiences in times of tranquility, ease, comfort, and peace, and it betrays any immaturity with anxiety and worry. Crisis squeezes our lives like a mighty bellows, and the hands that crisis uses are the left hand of worry and the right hand of anxiety. We are given two feet to counter those two hands: our left foot of trust and our right foot of obedience. These are the feet that wear the shoes of the Gospel of peace.

The laboratory of faith creates what we hope for. Like a master with his Stradivarius, the violin's brilliance is only seen and heard when the instrument is touched by a maestro whose hands have been prepared to make music into art.

Recently, leaders from every quarter of business, industry, and ministry—as well as from every continent on planet Earth—have been dealing simultaneously with unprecedented levels of stress. Anxiety and worry are at an all-time high.

In the restaurant industry alone, Fortune reports that more than 110,000 eating establishments closed due to the pandemic of 2020. This erased more than 2.5 million jobs in an industry that lost more than $240 billion in 2020. This may not seem alarming to you, but think about the fact that of those restaurants that closed because of COVID-19, 72 percent of the owners said they had closed for good. They admitted they would not be opening another restaurant in the future. Couple this with the fact that life has radically changed for restaurant patrons as well. Of the adults surveyed, 83 percent said that they would not be eating on premises in the foreseeable future. That's eight in ten adults. These statistics are devastating to the restaurateur if they view their future according to the paradigms of pre-COVID society.

But if the restaurant owner rises above the pressure of the crisis, they'll catch a thermal of creativity that will carry them to the stars. It is in the stratosphere of "macrovision" that the restaurateur can reimagine their business and, with a certain and sure hope, create new ways of achieving their dreams. Perspective shifts when a galactic view is obtained. Rise up until you can kick the stars.

For the restaurateur, instead of folding under the pressure of governmental guidelines that restrict operations and the anxiety of creating a safe space where customers will want to return to dine in person, what if they tackled the challenges of the crisis with a new imagination gained from a stratospheric perspective? What happens if the restauranteur reimagines how they will engage their customers? How can they streamline their operations and enjoy greater efficiency? How can they diversify their menu? How can they reignite their customer base and entice them to return to in-person dining?

The answer to the crisis, in which anxiety and worry are reigning, is not going to be something unknown; rather, it is our willingness to reimagine our future by seeing things differently. A new discovery may not be necessary, but innovation is.

The restaurateur must rise high enough to kick the stars. It's in the rarified air of creativity that they can address their fears, worries, anxieties, and stress by looking at new technology, different protocols, different services, and so on, all because they choose to rise in hope rather than to be crushed by the very real pressures of a crisis-laden world.

This book was written to inspire you to think differently. It was written to provoke you to see your life and your work from a different perspective. It is my prayer that you will be so empowered by its message that you celebrate your humanity while dancing among the stars. While you dance, kick the stars. Kick so high that you leap on the winged word of a certain promise—the place from which our hope springs eternal. It is among the stars that we are released from the pressures of performance to see where true success leads. There, we will all dance with the joy that comes from guaranteed success. Oh yes, there it's the only route to fly, it's the only highway to navigate, and it's the only boulevard to travel to get to the place where we are kicking the stars and embracing an uncertain future with certain hope!

2

Lessons Learned from a Mustang?

"With land come commands, with privilege comes responsibility!" This is the Lord's message to Moses in Deuteronomy 2.

The way we live determines the impact we have, and God has always intended His people to be an expression, a living example, of the people who worshipped the true and living God. God intended for Israel's worship to shape the people's lifestyles, inform their social justice, and form their community. This is the law of expression. This is God's love demonstrated. This is God revealed in holy community.

I'll never forget my first car! My father purchased a car to give to me as a sixteenth-birthday present. However, he wanted to give me a car that would be demonstrably different from the car he was given on his sixteenth birthday. He was given a '56 Chevy that was the talk of the town. For me, he wanted to ensure that my gift would be the type of car that could neither hurt me physically nor spoil me spiritually.

So, my father purchased me a Ford Mustang!

Now, I know that the mere mention of the Ford Mustang elicits images of the most provocative, sleek, powerful Shelby Mustang you can imagine.

Hold on. Don't get ahead of yourself. My car was no Shelby Mustang! In fact, it was quite the opposite. There was nothing sexy or sleek about this model of Mustang.

This car was a gift from the era when the Ford design team and engineering department had all suffered a mental meltdown, apparently. Ford had decided to depart from the rich tradition they had worked so hard to establish with their first-generation production of Mustangs.

My '76 Mustang was designed and built in that infamously painful period for American automakers when they were facing increasing emissions standards, nascent crash regulations, and rising fuel prices. It was at that moment they decided to abandon the stylish lines, the sporty coupé, and the long hood of the American legend: the Ford Mustang.

What had been one of Ford's top-selling cars of all time had suddenly met the end of its nostalgic glory.

The brilliant thing about it was that my father purchased the car for me for that specific reason. He was only too happy that the Ford design team had apparently been smoking weed instead of working for more such glory. He didn't mind that they had abandoned the iconic brand of their pony car.

Why? Because he was depending on its nominal power to keep me out of jail for speeding tickets or, worse, out of the hospital from using too much speed and horsepower. This new-era Mustang had an option: a four-cylinder or a six-cylinder engine. Wow—that was it. My car sounded like a rubber band being wound up on a balsa-wood airplane. It took thirty minutes to enter the on-ramp of the freeway.

My father, smart man that he is, knew that any time you transfer a blessing by gifting, you'd better make certain that said blessing doesn't become the recipient's curse: "With land come commands; with privilege comes responsibility!"

My dad was never that wrapped up in the gift itself; he was more interested in the other three keys that accompanied the car keys on the keyring.

My dad not only gave me a car; he also gave me my first business. On the car key ring were the keys to a six-bay car wash. He said, "I'm giving you this car as a gift; I'm giving you the car wash as your responsibility! If you take care to be a good steward of the car wash, maintaining it daily, you get to keep the car. If you mishandle your responsibility and fail to run this car wash business, you will forfeit your blessing and lose the car. You choose! Your work ethic is always about your choices, and it will be your choices that determine your future."

I was so happy about the car; I gladly accepted the responsibility. But in the ensuing years, when I got fatigued at the responsibility of my workload, I was motivated when I thought about losing the blessing that was supported by my stewardship. I hated the late nights and early mornings that the car wash demanded, but I loved the freedoms and privileges my Mustang afforded me.

My dad was as sly as a fox. He got me a car that would never reach eighty miles per hour and had the most horrid center console ever designed. He had no concern whatsoever that a female passenger could get too close to me and become a distraction. If I were to fixate on the reality that my car was the worst model of Mustang ever made, I would miss entirely the lesson that was given to me. It was never so much about the car as it was about my personal growth as a steward of blessings undeserved.

A distraction can spoil a blessing; a wrong choice can ruin a privilege. "A right word fitly spoken is like apples of gold in a network of silver" (Proverbs 25:11).

This world is filled with the noise of distractions and detractors, people determined to hate the many privileges they have been given, and despisers of the blessings they've inherited.

The cure for an ungrateful attitude is humility. The cure for an unthankful spirit is never forgetting the blessings our eyes have seen or letting them slip from our hearts as memories of godly privilege.

You see, no matter where we are today, or what trials we go through in this hour, His covenant of love for us is that He promised to stay close to us and that He would never leave us or forsake us: "The Lord our God is near us whenever we pray to Him" (Deuteronomy 4:7).

We should not curse our privilege. We should not waste our freedom. To disregard either of them is to lose them both. In aviation, the centerpiece of the instrument panel is the attitude indicator. The attitude indicator is the flight instrument that informs the pilot of the aircraft's orientation relative to Earth's horizon and gives an immediate indication of the smallest orientation change. There is a popular expression used by pilots when speaking of attitude that says, "Keep the blue side up." You see, the horizon line on the attitude indicator is definitive and clear: there is a horizon line with blue above and brown below, a miniature airplane, pitch lines that show whether the airplane is pointing up or down, and a bank angle with lines at 10, 20, 30, and 60 degrees to help the pilot "keep the blue side up."

As in aviation, our attitude determines our altitude. If our attitude is negative, we'll dive away from the sacred climes of possibility and crash into the ground below. But if our attitude is informed by God's Word, we'll soar into the stratosphere of unlimited possibility. It's in our daring, our faith-filled boldness, that we launch with our nose high, determined to rise and kick the stars.

3

What We Make Our First Proves Our Priority

I first encountered Jesus in a personal way in 1965. From that moment to this, I've learned that God's grace is sufficient, His love is unending, His mercies are new each morning, His judgments are sure, His peace is our bulwark, His righteousness is our glory, His faithfulness is our shield, and His compassion fails not!

In scripture, we discover the importance Jesus gives to our priorities and His instructions about how we should manage those priorities.

There are five times in scripture when "one thing" is noted: Psalm 27:4, Mark 10:21, Luke 10:42, John 9:25, and Philippians 3:13.

The psalmist says that the "one thing" we should seek is to "dwell in the House of the Lord"!

Mark records Jesus saying that the "one thing" needed was "passion for His glory."

Luke records Jesus saying that Mary has chosen the "one thing" needed.

John records the blind man saying, "One thing I know: I was blind, and now I see."

Paul, when writing to the Philippians, says, "The one thing I do, however, is to forget what is behind me and do my best to reach what is ahead."

The scriptures are replete with the significance and influence of priority.

Our priorities will bring us peace today and glory tomorrow, or our priorities will yield us strife today and deceit tomorrow. The difference is the choices we make under the influence of our priorities.

"Right Priority" is the operatic soloist who sings with great enthusiasm, "It is well with my soul!"

Ask yourself: What are my priorities? Is time with Jesus my priority? Do other things rule my affairs? Is my time filled with busyness? Is Jesus first in my life?

Make a schedule that puts Jesus first! Give Him your "firstfruits" of time! Make the first thing on your to-do list today the priority of His presence!

If you put Jesus first, you will enjoy His pleasures forevermore, and His presence will keep you in perfect peace in the midst of challenges, difficulties, trials, and tribulations. No matter the difficulty, He will be with you.

Today, it's my prayer that you will live the abundant life Jesus gives and that your new life will be an inspiration to others. As they see you putting Him first in your life, they'll be convinced to put Jesus first in their lives as well.

I pray that Jesus will give you the courage to stand up for the fallen, heal the broken, and help the hurting. May your worship put Him first. In His love, you will be filled with grace, and your testimony will bring fame to His name.

Prioritize—Jesus first!

The ultimate priority for humankind is to "Worship the Lord in the majesty of holiness" (Psalm 92:2).

The supreme duty of every person is to worship their Creator for time and eternity!

Worship is intensely practical, active, and dynamic. Worship is joyous. Worship is vibrant. Worship is transformative.

4

God Honors What Starts Small but Ends Well

Many times, I am approached by people who are interested in learning more about how my family came to faith. Our family's journey in faith began when Rev. William J. Seymour preached God's Word to my great-grandmother.

Convinced that the world was unraveling, the church was floundering, and the people of God were living far below the life God had promised them, he set out to preach them into a red-hot revival experience. It is said that the claims of this holy preacher created an atmosphere where the tangible presence of God was manifested—and the biblical evidence of the baptism of the Holy Spirit was seen and heard among all the people.

Pastor Seymour believed that the people needed to be filled with the power of the Holy Spirit, empowering them to be witnesses and preparing them for the imminent return of the Lord Jesus Christ.

Upon hearing Brother Seymour speaking about Jesus from Acts 2:4, my great-grandmother surrendered her heart and life to the Lord Jesus Christ and was baptized in the Holy Spirit. Soon afterward, Brother Seymour led my great-grandmother to the banks of a Houston bayou and baptized her there in the saving name of Jesus. Five generations later, his prayer still prevails, his preaching still lives, and His message still saves!

I'm very thankful for my heritage, and I am forever grateful to God for giving me a spiritual great-grandfather who refused to harbor the hurt, the pain, the bitterness, and the travails a son of slavery would have known if not for choosing Jesus. He said, "The color line is washed away in the Blood!" At a time when America was bitterly divided, God brought us a man who walked above, not beneath, and who believed racial harmony was achieved in the church, where all races and classes of people became one when "We are all baptized by one Spirit into one body" (1 Corinthians 12:13).

Today, Rev. William J. Seymour, the son of Louisiana slaves, who became the pastor of a small, humble Pentecostal mission on Azusa Street in Los Angeles, California, is considered the father of more than five hundred million believers around the world. Think of that: the message that Rev. William Seymour preached, and the work that he began at the Azusa Street mission, is now considered to be the origins of the second-largest family of Christians in the world.

I am reminded of the words of Zechariah:

> Do not despise the day of small beginnings, for the Lord rejoices to see the work begin, to see the plumb line in Zerubbabel's hand. (Zechariah 4:10)

The key to living a life free from bitterness is to silence the doubt that comes from the derby of people who "measure themselves by comparing themselves with themselves" (2 Corinthians 10:12). If you don't curse your insignificant beginning, God won't stop rejoicing over you in the end!

> Paul said, "And I am certain that God, who began the good work within you, will continue His work until it is finally finished on the day when Jesus Christ returns." (Philippians 1:6)

Remember those who came before you—and you'll be encouraged. You will see God's sovereignty ruling for you. You will see God working on your behalf. Be courageous, be strong, and tell the enemy that has marshaled their weaponry against you, "You won't prosper; I've come too far by faith!"

5

When We Feel Desperate

In my distress I cried out unto the Lord and He heard me.
—Jonah. 2:2

This statement is one of the most powerful statements in scripture. It sets apart the fact that the one true God of Abraham, Isaac, and Jacob is different from all other gods. I cry out … and He alone hears me!

All other gods are deaf; their wooden ears are unable to hear. Jesus, after having been on the Mountain of Transfiguration, descends with Peter, James, and John to, at once, be confronted with a desperate father's plea. The father cried out to Jesus, "Teacher, I beg You to look at my son, for he is my only child" (Luke 9:38).

> While he [the boy] was coming, the demon threw him to the ground and convulsed him. But Jesus rebuked the unclean spirit and healed the boy and gave him back to his father. And all were astonished at the majesty of God. But while they

were all marveling at everything he was doing,
Jesus said to His disciples. (Luke 9:42–43 ESV)

Did you see that? All were astonished at the majesty of God!

Marvel and majesty dance in the arena of confrontation. Only after there is a conflict or contest—only after our "cry for help" and "desperation of need" meet on the altar of our trust in God and obedience to His Word—do we see the fullest expressions of His agape love toward us.

Remember, no blessing goes uncontested because every blessing is designed to be the transport of God's majesty!

Don't curse the contest. Don't waste the need. Believe in the name of He who is our salvation: Jesus Christ of Nazareth!

6

The Royal Affair of
Love and Truth

Today, we are given a new opportunity to embrace our limitless possibilities and our extraordinary blessings with prayer and praise to the Lord, our Christ.

Truth becomes hard if it is not softened by love. Love becomes soft if it is not strengthened by truth.

Truth, love, trust, and obedience are the four poles that serve as the beams that frame the tepee. The skeletal structure on which all doctrine hangs is these four beams! The more truth we know, the more we love. The more truth we love, the more truth we obey. The more truth we obey, the more we trust God to rule over our lives.

When we consider the world in which we live, we are at once struck by the startling reality that this world is filled with lie-lovers and truth-haters. The twenty-four-hour news cycle is filled with fabrications and lies, manipulative stories, and make-believe lives.

It has been said that "comparison is the thief of joy," but it is the lack of love for truth that disqualifies us from God's love.

Why, you ask? Because "Love rejoices in Truth!" (1 Corinthians 13:4–7).

Truth reveals more of Jesus to us:

> Jesus said, "I am the Way and the Truth and the Life. No one comes to the Father except through Me!" (John 14:6)

The more we learn about Him, the more we are drawn to Him by the gravity of love. When we discover how much He loves us, our response should be greater love for Him! Love begets truth!

Love begets truth. Truth begets intimacy. Intimacy begets revelation. Revelation begets love. Love begets truth, birthing in us new insight through the truth revealed to us. That is the continuum of love and truth.

The more truth we see, the more we see Jesus. The more we see Him, the more we love Him.

Love "rejoices in the truth." While others may choose to greedily feast on evil rumors, slanderous reports, sensational newscasts, disasters, and destruction, love sweetly rejoices in the truth. Love rejoices with truth; in fact, it shares the joys of truth. When truth is denied or rejected, love finds no cause for rejoicing. Love is pure. Love is kindness in action—so it can never be unconcerned about or indifferent to morality. Love can only rejoice where truth triumphs. Jesus made truth the very essence of Christianity. In John 14:6, as well as Paul's letters to the Ephesians and Thessalonians, he writes, "We have heard of Him, and we have been taught by Him, because the Truth is in Jesus."

Paul went further:

> And with all deceivableness of unrighteousness in them that perish; because they received not the love of truth, that they might be saved. And for this cause God shall send them strong delusion,

that they should believe a lie: That they all might be damned who believe not the truth, but have pleasure in unrighteousness. (2 Thessalonians 2:10–12)

The aged apostle John, whose life was rich in God's truth, said, "I have no greater joy than this, to hear of my children walking in the truth" (3 John 4).

Henry Drummond famously said,

He who loves will love truth not less than men. He will rejoice in the truth—rejoice not in what he has been taught to believe; not in a particular church's polity or organization, in this or that; in this ism or in that ism; but "in the Truth." A Truth lover will only accept what is real; he/ she will strive to get at facts; he/she will search for truth with a humble and unbiased mind, and cherish whatever they find at any sacrifice.

The enemy desires to drive a wedge between truth and love by distorting God's Word so that they can introduce and ply their doubt. The devil wishes to confuse people about love by twisting the truth because it is by truth that we learn about God's nature and character, about His love and redemption, and about His grace and His mercy!

Jesus's own prayer in the Garden of Gethsemane was that "His Father would protect His followers from the devil and teach them the Truth about God's Word!" (John 17:13–19).

Scripture also teaches us that we are to ambitiously "guard our hearts" by taking an offensive position (a football analogy) regarding our response: being proactive with regard to truth. We are to "guard our hearts" against lies, deceit, and the spirits of darkness by proclaiming the "Truth in Love" (Ephesians 4:11–15).

When we "speak the truth in love, we will grow up into Jesus in all things, which is the Head, even Christ!" (Ephesians 4:15).

The summum bonum of Christianity is the superlative spiritual gift of love. It is love that teaches us truth from our Father's perspective—the perspective of love: "God is love" (1 John 4:8).

Paul, in his epistles, had previously presented the Christian faith with analogies of a building and a body, but in his Corinthian letter, he expresses love as the one thing in which all the varied parts find their unity and meaning: in the all-embracing love of God.

Adolf von Harnack said that 1 Corinthians 13 was "the greatest, strongest, deepest, thing Paul ever wrote."

Every person has, at one time or another in their life, asked themselves, "What is the greatest, the most essential, the most important, and the most real and enduring thing in life and the universe?"

Some of the greatest thinkers in human history, in all ages, have asked and answered this question.[1]

Plato said, "The highest good is justice," which he defined as having and doing what is one's own—a social responsibility as well as personal privilege.

Aristotle answered that this highest good is found in the golden mean, or the aurea mediocritas, the middle of the way. Thus, moderation is his answer.

Heraclitus thought it was found in a combination and unification of opposites that results in a harmonious whole.

Socrates thought he had found it in a universal, innate knowledge in human nature, which, when people recognized it, would cause us automatically to do what we knew to be right. He said, "Virtue is knowledge"— knowledge in action. To know is to do.

The Stoics thought that the highest good was conformity to

---

[1] King, R. (2021). "More Than 110,000 Eating and Drinking Establishments Closed in 2020." *Fortune.* https://fortune. com/2021/01/26/restaurants-bars-closed-2020-jobs-lost-how-ma- ny-have-closed-us-covid-pandemic-stimulus-unemployment.

the harmony of the universe—a sort of fatalistic submission to the harmony of the universe, not unlike that of Islam.

Philo and Plotinus saw it in the good soul's ultimate release from the body of evil matter.

Saint Augustine saw it in the soul's final union with God—when the absence of all evil will be realized.

Immanuel Kant, the great German philosopher, thought he had found the highest good in a sort of negative Golden Rule:

> Always act in such a way that the maxim determining your conduct might well become a universal law; act so that you can will that everybody shall follow the principle of your action.

God answered this question for the ancient Israelites in the commandments given to them through Moses. The Ten Commandments spelled out for the Israelites what Paul was talking about in 1 Corinthians 13.

Jesus epitomized the Ten Commandments, reducing them to two all-embracing commandments, converting them from the negative to the positive, and making them the very essence of Christianity (see Luke 10:25–28; Romans 13:10).

Christianity alone provides both the ideal of the highest good and the inner enabling of the realization of that good. In 1 Corinthians, Paul explains that the possession and practice of love towers above all other human gifts or abilities.

Drummond concluded: "Love and Truth are not things born of enthusiastic emotion. Love is the rich, strong, vigorous expression of Christ's Gospel—it is Christ-like nature in its fullest development!"

7

A Thing to Pray and a Thing to Remember

It is the wise who start each day praying for the protection of the Lord. We are to pray for His love and His truth to safeguard us.

It has often been said that the mountaintops of life are given to inspire us, but it's in the valleys of life that we grow in maturity.

Mountaintops are made for those moments that can transfigure our thinking, and the valleys are made to expose us to the tough realities of life.

The disciples of Jesus found that it was in the valleys that they met their own failures in ministry. It was at the bottom that they were able to rightly discern their lack of spiritual understanding. It was in the valleys of life that the disciples experienced anxieties born out of their inexperience. It was in the valleys they learned how to avoid foolish rivalries.

When Jesus took His beloved disciples up to the Mount of Transfiguration, He did so to allow them to see with clarity the reality of life in the valley from an entirely different perspective: a heavenly perspective.

With a heavenly perspective and a right relationship with eternal truth, Jesus calls His followers to an all-embracing love. Today, Jesus continues to call us—you and me—to welcome people:

> Whoever welcomes this little child in My Name welcomes Me; and whoever welcomes Me welcomes the One who sent Me. (Luke 9:48)

When we determine to view our valleys from a heavenly perspective, the eyes of our understanding are opened, and what we see by the spirit of wisdom and revelation informs us of the glories to come on our mountain.

It was in the Garden of Gethsemane, His valley of death, that Jesus kept His eye on a future upper room. It was His vision that anchored His faith in the will of God, and it was His vision that formed His experience. Experience informs our understanding with insight, and as a result, that knowledge anticipates the coming of a new mountaintop (or upper room) experience.

It's this continuum:

> Heavenly perspective —> view of the valley —> opens understanding —> informs vision —> grants wisdom —> reveals new strategies —> reveals new glories in the cosmic mountains, the playground of the stars.

The beginning is the Hebrew letter Aleph, the letter whose very construction starts in the heavens. The plight of humanity starts in the valley of sin and despair, but the visionary of redemption is informed of the manifold wisdom of God robed in flesh, which reveals the glory of a "new creation" mountaintop, where all things are absolutely, unequivocally, made new.

8

Our Sure Hope

We can never defeat what we will not confront; we will never overcome what we pretend does not exist.

Truth is not an opinion formed in the galaxy of our personal choice, and it is not found in the whims of pragmatism or skepticism. Truth is absolute. Truth is firm. Truth is never based on someone's opinions, ideas, or beliefs. Truth is in God because God is truth! God's Word is absolute because it is unchanging, unmovable, inerrant, and infallible.

Today, the world is witnessing a nation unmoored, reeling from a tsunami of crises. A pandemic, economic instability, strife, protests, social isolation, grief, uncertainty, sadness, and sorrow all drive media propaganda to incessantly promote fear, isolation, and turmoil. As a result, fear—not faith—is driving many in our nation straight into the perils of distress.

There is hope for pandemic dwellers. It is the Word of God:

> Sanctify them through Thy truth: Thy word is truth. (John 17:17).

The sum of Your word is truth, And every one of Your righteous ordinances is everlasting. (Psalm 119:160)

Now, O Lord God, You are God, and Your words are truth, and You have promised this good thing to Your servant. (2 Samuel 7:28)

Sanctify them in the truth; Your word is truth. (John 17:1)

Then the woman said to Elijah, "Now I know that you are a man of God and that the word of the Lord in your mouth is truth." (1 Kings 17:24)

The fear of the Lord is clean, enduring forever; The judgments of the Lord are true; they are righteous altogether. (Psalm 19:9)

And do not take the word of truth utterly out of my mouth, For I wait for Your ordinances. (Psalm 119:43)

You are near, O Lord, And all Your commandments are truth. (Psalm 119:151)

By the word of truth, by the power of God; by the weapons of righteousness for the right hand and the left. (2 Corinthians 6:7)

Your righteousness is an everlasting righteousness, And Your Word is truth. (Psalm 119:142)

And they sent their disciples to Him, along with the Herodians, saying, "Teacher, we know that You are truthful and teach the way of God in truth, and defer to no one; for You are not partial to any." (Matthew 22:16)

They came and said to Him, "Teacher, we know that You are truthful and defer to no one; for You are not partial to any, but teach the way of God in truth. Is it lawful to pay a poll-tax to Caesar, or not?" (Mark 12:14)

They questioned Him, saying, "Teacher, we know that You speak and teach correctly, and You are not partial to any, but teach the way of God in truth." (Luke 20:21)

Therefore Pilate said to Him, "So You are a king?" Jesus answered, "You say correctly that I am a king. For this I have been born, and for this I have come into the world, to testify to the truth. Everyone who is of the truth hears My voice." (John 18:37)

There is another who testifies of Me, and I know that the testimony which He gives about Me is true. (John 5:32)

An instructor of the foolish, a teacher of the immature, having a form of knowledge and of truth in the Law. (Romans 2:20)

But we did not yield in subjection to them for even an hour, so that the truth of the Gospel would remain with you. (Galatians 2:5)

In Him, you also, after listening to the message of truth, the Gospel of your salvation—having also believed, you were sealed in Him with the Holy Spirit of promise. (Ephesians 1:13)

For the hope which is laid up for you in heaven, whereof you previously heard in the word of truth, the Gospel. (Colossians 1:5)

All scripture is inspired by God and profitable for teaching, for reproof, for correction, for training in righteousness. (2 Timothy 3:16)

On the other hand, I am writing a new commandment to you, which is true in Him and in you, because the darkness is passing away and the true Light is already shining. (1 John 2:8)

And He who sits on the throne said, "Behold, I am making all things new." And He said, "Write, for these words are faithful and true." (Revelation 21:5)

And He said to me, "These words are faithful and true"; and the Lord, the God of the spirits of the prophets, sent His angel to show to His bond-servants the things which must soon take place. (Revelation 22:6)

Then the king said to him, "How many times must I adjure you to speak to me nothing but the truth in the name of the Lord?" (Kings 22:16)

The vision of the evenings and mornings which has been told is true; But keep the vision secret, For it pertains to many days in the future. (Daniel 8:26)

Thy word is a lamp unto my feet, and a light unto my path. (Psalm 119:105)

All scripture is given by inspiration of God, and is profitable for doctrine, for reproof, for correction, for instruction in righteousness: That the man of God may be perfect, thoroughly furnished unto all good works. (Timothy 3:16–17)

For the prophecy came not in old time by the will of man: but holy men of God spake as they were moved by the Holy Ghost. (2 Peter 1:21)

God, who at sundry times and in divers manners spake in time past unto the fathers by the prophets. (Hebrews 1:1)

As he spake by the mouth of this holy prophets which have been since the world began. (Luke 1:70)

And this is the record, that God hath given to us eternal life, and this life is in his son. (1 John 5:11)

He that rejecteth Me, and receiveth not My words hath one that judgeth him: the word that I have spoken, the same shall judge him in the last day. For I have not spoken of myself; but the Father which sent Me, He gave me a commandment, what I should say, and what I should speak. (John 12:48–49)

There is insurmountable evidence that the Bible is the record of God's redemption of humanity in all dispensations—with all its different conditions. The scriptures are the Word of God, and the Word of God is truth:

> Truth (אֱמֶת, emeth; ἀλήθεια, alētheia): Factuality, faithfulness, firmness, reality, reliability.

In the Old Testament, the most common term for "truth" is אֱמֶת (emeth). The semantic range of אֱמֶת (emeth) includes factuality and validity as well as faithfulness, firmness, and reliability. In the Septuagint, it is most often translated using ἀλήθεια (alētheia); πίστις (pistis) or δικαιοσύνη (dikaiosynē) are also occasionally used. Truth can be predicated on people as well as propositions.

When truth is used in a factual sense, אֱמֶת (emeth) indicates a genuine state of affairs as opposed to a false one. It is used in Deuteronomy, in the context of a legal investigation (Deuteronomy 13:14; 17:4; 22:20). In Daniel 10:1, "truth" is used to describe the word that Daniel received in a vision. It can also be used as an indication of honesty in speech:

- The queen of Sheba discovered that the reports she had heard about Solomon were factual (1 Kings 10:6–7).
- The widow of Zarephath told Elijah after he raised her son from the dead that "the word of the Lord in your mouth is truth" (1 Kings 17:24 NRSV).
- The king of Israel insisted that Micaiah tell the truth when he prophesied (1 Kings 22:16; 2 Chron. 18:15).
- The one who can dwell in the Lord's sanctuary is one who tells the truth (Psalm 15:2).
- Zechariah prophesied to the returned exiles that they ought to speak the truth to one another (Zech. 8:16).

In the Old Testament, truth is also understood as faithfulness and reliability, and ת מֶ אֶ (emeth) frequently occurs together with חסד (chsd), "mercy," to indicate God's loyalty to people (Genesis 24:27; 32:10; Exodus 34:6; 2 Samuel 2:6; Psalms 25:10; 61:7; 89:14; Micah 7:20).

- God's ת מֶ אֶ (emeth) is contrasted with the wrongdoing of his people (Neh. 9:33).
- The works of his hands are ת מֶ אֶ (emeth), in the sense of faithfulness (Psalm 111:7–8).
- God's promise to David "from which he will not turn back" is described as ת מֶ אֶ (emeth) (Psalm 132:11 NRSV).
- People are also described as ת מֶ אֶ (emeth) in the sense of faithfulness or reliability (Exodus 18:21; Joshua 2:14; Nehemiah 7:2).

In the New Testament, we see terms associated with truth such as ἀλήθεια (aletheia, "truth"), ἀληθής (alethes, "true"), ἀληθινός (alethinos, "true," "real"), ἀληθεύω (aletheuo, "to tell the truth"), and ἀληθῶς (alethos, "truly"). These words are used in three senses:

- To convey a sense of being factual, as opposed to being false or in error. This is the dominant sense of "truth" in the New Testament. Frequent uses include:
  - To characterize a quality of speech indicating honesty or sincerity (Mark 5:33; John 4:18; 8:40; 16:7; Acts 26:25; 2 Corinthians 7:14; 12:6).
  - To contrast telling the truth with lying (Romans 9:1; Ephesians 4:25; 1 Timothy 2:7).
  - To describe the Gospel (2 Corinthians 4:2; Galatians 2:5, 14; Ephesians 1:13; Colossians 1:5; Hebrews 10:26; 3 John 3–4).
- To indicate faithfulness or reliability, as used in the New Testament in Romans 3:4, 7, and 15:8.

- To describe reality—that which is real and genuine as opposed to fake or only an imitation. It also describes that which is complete versus incomplete.
  - Jesus is the true light (John 1:9).
  - The Father desires true worshipers (John 4:23–24).
  - Jesus's body is true food (John 6:32, 55).
  - Jesus is the true vine (John 15:1).
  - The truth of God is exchanged for a lie (Romans 1:25).
  - Jesus ministers in the true tabernacle (Hebrews 8:2; 9:24).
  - Love must be performed not with words, but in truth (1 John 3:18).
  - Jesus is the most significant figure in human history.
  - Jesus claimed to be more than a religious leader. He claimed to be the "way, the truth, the life." It is evident from His claims that He considered Himself to be the Son of God.
  - Jesus leaves us with only three possibilities: He was a fraud. He was insane. Or He was who He said He was—God.

The Bible is the Word of God, and there is adequate proof that the Bible is God's record for us. Therefore, it is incumbent upon us to seek out the truth of God's Word that was given to us for our salvation. A person who is investigating the claims of Jesus must seek His Word with an open mind and heart so as to understand His promises and provisions, His commands, His covenants, His laws, and His statutes. We should always be at the ready to take up the only visible weapon that Jesus has given to us and win the victory in this last day and age of the New Testament Church.

The English word *Bible* is derived from the Greek *biblion* and *biblos* meaning "roll" or "book." A biblion was a roll of papyrus made of *byblus*—a reedlike plant whose inner bark was dried and fashioned into a writing material widely used in the ancient world.

The Bible was originally written in three languages: Hebrew, Aramaic, and Greek. The Old Testament was written almost completely in Hebrew, the language spoken by the Israelites in Canaan before the Exile. After their return, however, the common speech gradually gave way to Aramaic. Parts of Daniel and Ezra and one verse of Jeremiah (10:11) are in Aramaic. Aramaic was the vernacular of Palestine spoken by the common class in New Testament times. This is understood to have been the language that Jesus used in His teaching. Afterward, it was translated into Greek by the writers of the early Apostolic Church (see "Aramaic Language").

The Bible contains history, law, biography, prophecy, and poetry. It is similar in many ways to other books, yet it is set apart from all other literary works in that it is the only book to have God as its author. Although the meaning of the word *Bible* is ecclesiastical in origin, its roots go back to the Old Testament. Daniel 9:2 (LXX) (*ta biblia*) refers to the prophetic writings. In the prologue to Sirach, it refers generally to the Old Testament scriptures. This usage passed into the Christian Church, and at about the turn of the fifth century, it was extended to include the entire body of canonical writings as we now have them. The expression *ta biblia* passed into the vocabulary of the Western Church, and in the thirteenth century, by what Brooke Foss Westcott calls a "happy solecism" (*The Bible in the Church*, 5). The neuter plural came to be regarded as a feminine singular, and in this form, the term passed into the languages of modern Europe. This significant change, from plural to singular, reflected the growing conception of the Bible as an utterance of God rather than a multitude of voices speaking for Him.

The process by which the various books in the Bible were brought together and recognized as sacred scripture is referred to as the "history of the canon." Contrary to prevailing critical opinion, there existed prior to the Exile, a large body of sacred literature. Moses wrote, "All the words of the Lord" in the "book of the covenant" (Exodus 21--23, 24:4). Joshua's farewell address was written in the "book of the law of God" (Joshua 24:26). Samuel spoke concerning the manner of the kingdom and "wrote it in a book" (1 Samuel 10:25). "Thus saith the Lord" was a common preface to the utterances of the prophets.

This revelatory literature was regarded from the very beginning as the revealed will of God and was therefore binding upon the people. The "oracles of God" were held in highest esteem, and this attitude toward the scriptures was naturally carried over into the early church. Few critics deny that Jesus regarded the Old Testament as the inspired record of God's self-revelation in history.

Jesus Christ repeatedly appealed to the scriptures as authority (Matthew 19:4; 22:29). The early church maintained this same attitude toward the Old Testament, but, along with it, they began to place the Word of the Lord within the context of their present predicaments. While the Old Testament canon had been formally closed, the coming of Christ had, in a sense, opened it again—God was once again speaking. Since the cross was the most efficacious redemptive act of God in history, the New Testament became a logical necessity. Thus, the voices of the apostles, and later, their writings, were accepted as the Divine commentary on the life of Jesus Christ.

Within the first century, various epistles began to be written; as they were penned, they began to be read and circulated among the churches. Marcion, one of the most famous Gnostics in this period, began to advocate heresies that demanded some Christian authority. With all these intruding evils attempting to seed themselves among the early Christians, there was a definite need to know what was going on here in order to be received as the apostolic writings. Out of this came what we know today as the New Testament canon. At the Council of Carthage in AD 397, the canon (New Testament) was ultimately certified.

The Bible's claim of divine origins is justified by its historical influence. Its manuscripts are numbered in the thousands. The New Testament had barely been put together before we found translations in Latin, Syriac, and Egyptian. Today, there is no language in the civilized world that does not have a translation of the Word of God. No other book has been so carefully studied, discussed, or covered. Its spiritual influence cannot be overestimated. It is preeminently the Book: "God's Word in man's language" (*Baker's Dictionary of Theology*, 94).

Aramaic appears to have been the common language of the Savior and of His early disciples, yet it is not the language of the New Testament. This may be of some concern to a few. Therefore, I will attempt to offer information that should dispel some doubt.

The most appropriate language to help propagate the Christian Gospel is the one that was used by the people at the time. Greek fulfilled this need like no other language. When the Gospel began to be proclaimed, it was the Greek language that was considered the international language. This language was spoken around the Aegean shore, in the eastern Mediterranean, and in other areas. The Greek-speaking Jewish believers are mentioned in the sixth chapter of Acts. The Old Testament was written in the language of those to whom it was sent: Hebrew. The new Covenant that the Lord made with his followers was to be proclaimed to all the world. Therefore, if this was the objective, the language that would fulfill this purpose would be the language employed by our Lord. For tender expressiveness and flexibility, classical Greek is unsurpassed. I offer the following to support my point:

> No competent judge can dispute the claim of Greek to preeminence in any congress of languages, ancient or modern. In its Golden prime it presents an unrivalled combination of elegance and vigor of variety of style and precision of statement. "The instrument responds," remarks Jebb, "with happy elasticity to every demand of the Greek intellect." And when we call to mind the felicities of its characteristic idioms, the repleteness of its

syntax, the intricate harmonies of its prosody, and the sonorous cadence of its statelier prose, or reflect on the copious invention exhibited in its teeming vocabulary; and then bethink ourselves of the monumental longevity of the tongues, the siege of time it has sustained without capitulation; the title of Greek to homage in any symposium of the common wealth of letters must be fully conceded.[2]

Palestine became a part of the Roman Empire in 63 BC, as part of the province of Syria. At this time, Greek was the common language of those regions as well as of the eastern Roman Empire generally. The Roman Empire was considered bilingual. The Roman army spoke Latin officially, and it was considered the official language of the Empire, but, at the same time, Greek remained the official language around the eastern Mediterranean. Greek was spoken as much in the city of Rome—as was Latin—by the highest as well as the lowest classes. Greek was considered the language of the educated and cultured. Often, slaves were largely Greek speaking by birth, and it appears the early Christian believers of Rome were Greek speaking as well. The epistle to the early Roman believers was written to them in Greek; no doubt, Paul could have just as easily penned the letter in Latin. The Greek language held predominance among the Roman believers until about the beginning of the third century.

Until about 150 years ago, it was thought that the Greek in which the New Testament was written was referred to as the "language of the Holy Ghost," but, of course, research and archaeology have changed this idea. The "language of the Holy Ghost" turned out to be the language spoken by the common people of that day. Dr. Lightfoot gave this reference in a lecture concerning a word in the

---

[2] E. K. Simpson, F. N. Bruce, *The Books and the Parchments*, 60.

New Testament that was not found in classical Greek outside the fifth century:

> You are not to suppose that the word had fallen out of use in the interval, only that it had not been used in the books which remain to us; probably it had been part of the common speech all along. I will go further and say, that if we could only recover letters that ordinary people wrote to each other without any thought of being literary, we should have the greatest possible help for the understanding of the language of the New Testament generally.[3]

> It was not long before this remarkable prophecy was put to the test. From the 1880s onward, large numbers of the very sort of thing that Lightfoot desired—letters and other documents written by ordinary people, from the centuries immediately preceding and following the time of Christ—have come to light after two millennia of burial in the sands of Egypt. Many of these are written on scraps of papyrus and pieces of pottery (ostraca). These vernacular documents, recovered from ancient rubbish dumps, proved to be written in a kind of Greek strikingly similar to the Greek of the New Testament. The "language of the Holy Ghost" turned out to be the language of the common people, which is just what we should expect.[4]

The purpose of studying the Bible is to know God and to discover our responsibility to Him. Upon discovering His Word of life given to us, if we trust and obey the words we have received,

---

[3] J. H. Moulton, *Prolegommena* (1908), 242.

[4] F. F. Bruce, *The Books and the Parchments*, 63–64.

we will live our lives accordingly—with the joy of knowing that we are pleasing the Lord God.

A good place to begin our studies is in the first four words of the Bible: "In the beginning God." That is the origin of all that we know, see, and have today; all reasons for the Earth, sea, constellations, galaxies, humanity, animal kingdom, birds, and any inanimate substance is God. Everything centers on God.

Another reason for learning scripture and teaching it to others is so they may know the Lord. The Lord's overall objective for the church is to evangelize the world—that "whosoever will may come." The Gospel dispensation is based on voluntary service; it is not done by law or by coercion.

God is looking for the willing and obedient—those who have placed their faith and trust in Him—to make up His great spiritual army, which is on its pilgrimage through this world.

If we come to know the Book and fail to know the Lord of the Book, the purpose of God has not been realized in us and the purpose of God in the Book has been defeated. This Book, the Bible, is God's prescribed will for humanity, so there will be no conflict between us and God. We must study the Bible:

- The Bible is a holy book (see 2 Timothy 2:15).
- The Bible is God's voice (see Hebrews 1:1).
- The Bible is light (see Psalm 119:105).
- The Bible is a revelation (see Revelation 1:1–3).

The word "revealed" denotes something brought forth that was hidden, something made plain that was obscure, and something enlightened that was dark.

Humanity is the only thing that God made in His image; all else bore no similarity to God or His nature. Humans can think, imagine, dream, and long. We long to know from whence we came, our purpose in being here, and where we will go from here. This is the ontological philosophy. All human knowledge at best breaks down here, and what faint light it throws on this is like the spark of a flint compared to the shining sun.

The Bible comes in like a roaring Niagara with the revelation of its author—the Creator of humanity—of our purpose and our future. The Bible reveals God to us and gives us an insight into ourselves. Only the true God of this universe could furnish such marvelous information as is written in the Bible. This demands an omniscient intelligence. The darkness becomes light, the hidden becomes clearly seen, and the misunderstood becomes understood. It declares to humanity the how, and it equips us for the journey of our earthly pilgrimage.

9

The Divine Guide for Travelers to the Stars

And that from a child you have known the holy scriptures,
which are able to make you wise unto salvation through
faith which is in Jesus Christ. All scripture is given by
inspiration of God, and is profitable for doctrine, for reproof,
for correction, for instruction in righteousness. That the man
of God may be thoroughly furnished unto all good works.
—2 Timothy 3:15–17

As a light and a revelation, the Bible is the highest spiritual authority
to guide us on our pathways. There are some things in life in which
we dare not make a mistake: how we are to be saved, the way in
which we are saved, and God's requirements of us for Him to count
us as right and saved.

We must be "positionally" made right so that no sin will be
imputed to us. For this information to be available, we must first
know our needs, know the end from the beginning, and know
what it will take for us to make heaven our home. This scriptural

knowledge is intended to be sufficient for our salvation, protecting us from any error that could affect our eternal destiny. Our heavenly Father has provided this knowledge to us in the Word of God.

The prophecies of the Old Testament vaguely speak of some of the great truths of the New Testament, but as Divine inspiration is continually given and received, making complete the revelation of God, they become more clearly understood. With the unfolding of the New Testament, humanity is able to see the purpose of the coming of Jesus Christ, as He was and is the last sacrifice for sin.

In the book of Revelation, we see humanity glorified and made in the image of the Creator. In the foreknowledge of God, it was God's purpose to bring humanity to glorification. The book of Revelation is a complete panoramic view of the Creator and His relationship to us, the blessing if we obey the message of Jesus Christ, and the curse if we do not. Thank the Lord for His revelation to us.

10

The Bible and Its Effect on Civilization

Among all the religions by which people endeavor to worship, Christianity is the most widespread, has the most adherents, and has the most remarkable claims for the divinity of its founder and the finality of its teachings. Of the 7.8 billion human beings on Earth in 2020, more than 2.4 billion identified as Christians.

Inevitably, some questions arise: From where did the Christian religion come? How did it spread? From the days of St. Luke—who wrote his account of the Acts of the Apostles in the first Christian century—down to the present, thousands of scholars have labored to tell this story. All these writers and scholars use the Bible as their basis: God's written Word. There is nothing more powerful than the Word of God:

> All scripture is given by inspiration of God, and is profitable for doctrine, for reproof, for correction, for instruction in righteousness. (2 Timothy 3:16)

Inspiration comes from the Greek word *theopneustos*, which means "God-breathed." God supernaturally inspired and directed the writing of scripture in order that He might, with absolute accuracy, give to humanity His comprehensive and infallible revelation for our redemption. This was one of the strong impetuses that converted the Roman Empire from paganism to Christianity in the days of the apostle Paul. Christianity became the religion of the Roman Empire in a short period of time.

The New Testament has shaped civilization more decisively than anything else ever written. Its twenty-seven varied documents, largely compiled between the years AD 50 and AD 100, tell of the beginnings of Christianity.

To accurately understand the power and influence of the Bible on civilization, we must look at it at the macro level, thus getting a panoramic view of its authority and influence.

The Bible is one book. There are seven markers that make this declaration of unity.

- In Genesis, the Bible bears witness to one God, and we know that one God to be Jesus Christ manifested in flesh. When God speaks, He is consistent with Himself and with the total revelation concerning Him.
- The Bible forms one continuous story—the relationship of humanity to God.
- The Bible records some of the most unlikely predictions, and when time has elapsed, it records their fulfillment.
- The Bible is a graduating scale of unfolding truth. Everything is not told at once, and once for all. The Law is "first the blade, then the ear, after that the full corn." There might be centuries between the writers; then a different writer will pick up the same subject and continue without contradicting the other, each not knowing the other, then another until the full picture is complete.

- From the beginning to the end, the Bible testifies of one redemption, and this redemption came about by Jesus Christ our Lord.
- The Bible testifies on one great theme: the person and work of Jesus Christ.
- Finally, the writers, some forty-four in number, writing over twenty centuries, have produced a harmonious doctrine. This should be to every candid mind the necessary proof of the infallibility of scripture and its divine inspiration.

The Bible is a Book of books. Sixty-six books make up the one Book. Each book, when speaking of unity, could be considered a chapter, although each book has its own theme and is complete within itself. Each book should be studied in the light of its distinctive theme. Genesis is considered a book of beginnings; Exodus, a book of redemption; Leviticus, a book of priesthood ordinances and righteousness; etc.

The books of the Bible also fall into groups. Speaking in a broad sense, the Bible can be arranged into five divisions. Christ is the theme of each of these divisions:

- Old Testament—preparation
- Gospels—manifestation
- Acts—propagation
- Epistles—explanation
- Revelation—consummation

In other words, the Old Testament is a preparation for the coming of Christ, giving the seeker of truth and faith information about who to believe in and what to believe, looking forward to the cross. In the Gospels, Jesus Christ is manifested to the world. In Acts, which is a history of the early church, the Gospel of Christ is spread to the world. In the Epistles, the Gospel is explained. In Revelation, all things are consummated in and through Jesus Christ.

The Old Testament can be classified into four groups:

Law
Genesis
Exodus
Leviticus
Numbers
Deuteronomy

History
Joshua
1 and 2 Kings
Esther
Judges
1 and 2 Chronicles
Ruth
Ezra
1 and 2 Samuel
Nehemiah

Poetry
Job
Proverbs
Song of Solomon
Psalms
Ecclesiastes
Lamentations

Prophecy
Isaiah
Jeremiah
Ezekiel
Daniel
Hosea
Joel
Amos
Obadiah
Jonah
Micah
Nahum
Habakkuk
Zephaniah
Haggai
Zechariah
Malachi

In the New Testament, we have this group:

Gospels
Matthew
Mark
Luke
John

History
Acts
Epistles
Romans
1 and 2 Corinthians

Galatians	Hebrews
Ephesians	James
Philippians	1 and 2 Peter
Colossians	1, 2, and 3 John
1 and 2 Thessalonians	Jude
1 and 2 Timothy	
Titus	**Prophecy**
Philemon	Revelation

The Bible tells the story of humanity. Beginning with the creation of the Earth and human beings, the Bible tells the story of how the human race began from Adam and Eve. This story is continued through the first eleven chapters.

Then, beginning with the twelfth chapter, the story of Abraham is told, which declares that he was the progenitor of the nation of Israel.

The Gentiles are only mentioned when they are connected with Israel. Some have asked why. In Deuteronomy 7:7–10, the explanation is given. God had four main reasons for selecting Israel as He did:

- To prove to the world there is only one God in a world of idolatry.
- To prove the blessing of serving that one true and living God.
- To receive, transmit, and preserve the scriptures.
- To provide the posterity from which the Messiah should come.

The biblical story of Israel can be separated into eight sections:

- From the call of Abraham to the deliverance from Egyptian bondage (Genesis 12; Exodus 14:30).
- From Egypt to the death of Joshua (Exodus 21; Joshua 24).

- From the death of Joshua to the first monarch, Saul.
  - The period of the kings to the captivity in Babylon.
  - The seventy years of captivity in Babylon.
  - The restored kingdom until the destruction of Jerusalem in AD 70.
  - The dispersion after AD 70.
  - From AD 70 until the present regathering when Israel became a nation: May 15, 1948.

The Gospels record the coming of Jesus Christ (the Messiah of the Jews) and His rejection, Crucifixion, resurrection, and ascension.

Acts records the descent of the Holy Spirit into the heart of each believer. This was a new thing in human history. The New Testament Church was born in AD 33 with twelve apostles. Some of these apostles were writers of the New Testament. The New Testament was a product of the church.

Israel was in the foreground from the time of Abraham until the resurrection of Christ. Now, the church comes on the scene and is predominant until the fourth chapter of Revelation. From the fourth chapter of the book of Revelation until its fulfillment, we are presented with the final reign of Jesus Christ over all the nations of the world.

The central theme of the Bible is Christ. The deity of Jesus Christ, God manifested in flesh, His death, His resurrection, and His ascension all constitute the Gospel (1 Timothy 3:16).

The Gospel preached in Acts is further explained in the Epistles. Jesus was the Son of God, Son of man, Son of Abraham, and Son of David, which provides one central theme for the whole Bible.

Jesus Christ is the seed of woman that destroys the seed of Satan. He is the seed of Abraham that became the Earth blessed, the seed of David in that He reigns as Israel's king. He is God in human form, and in that, He became the head of the church, which is His body on earth. As the church, we are looking forward with great expectation to His anticipated return. The first chapter of the book of Revelation states "The Revelation of Jesus Christ." No matter which direction you turn in the Bible, the shadow of Calvary falls across your path.

11

Notable Quotes and Sayings about the Bible

Abraham Lincoln

> I believe the Bible is the best gift God has ever given to Man. All the good from the Savior of the world is communicated to us through this Book.

George Washington

> It is impossible to rightly govern the world without the Bible.

Thomas Carlyle

> The Bible is the truest utterance that ever came by alphabetic letters from the soul of man, through which, as though a window divinely opened, all

men could look into the stillness of eternity, and discern in glimpses their far distant, long-forgotten home.

Henry Van Dyke

Born in the East and clothed in oriental form and imagery, the Bible walks the ways of all the world with familiar feet and enters land after land to find its own everywhere. It has learned to speak in hundreds of languages to the heart of man. Children listen to its stories with wonder and delight, and wise men ponder them as parables of life. The wicked and proud tremble at its warnings, but to the wounded and penitent it has a mother's voice. It has woven itself into our dearest dreams, so that love, friendship, sympathy, devotion, memory, hope, put on the beautiful garments of its treasured speech. No man is poor or desolate who has this treasure of his own. When the landscape darkens and the trembling pilgrim comes to the valley named of the Shadow, he is not afraid to enter; he takes the rod and staff of scripture in his hand; he says to friend and comrade, "Goodbye; we shall meet again," and confronted by that support, he goes toward the lonely pass as one who walks through darkness into light.

Josephus

There was about this time Jesus, a doer of wonderful works.

12

Developing a Deeply Rooted Confidence That God Exists and That He Is Good

The apostle Paul urges us to "rejoice in the Lord always!" (Philippians 4:4). Paul understood that his admonition to all of us that we should "rejoice in the Lord" provokes us to make a decision. This is a decision that has to come from a deeply rooted confidence that God is good, that He is in control, and that He is working out our salvation.

God is good! God's goodness has provided for us His Word. His Word has come to us because of His goodness and love for us. God's Word is given to us for our very own good. William Moorehead offers the following in his notable work, *The Typology of Scripture*:

> A "type" is a draft or sketch of some well-defined feature of redemption, and therefore it must distinctly resemble its antitype. Aaron the High Priest is a rough figure of Jesus our Great High

Priest. A type always looks to the future; an element of revelation is in it.

In Deuteronomy, Moses writes to Israel (a type of the New Testament Church) regarding the Lord's requirements for Israel:

> And now, Israel, what does the Lord require of you, but to fear the Lord your God, to walk in His ways, and to love Him, and to serve the Lord your God with all your heart and with all your soul. To keep the commandments [Word] of the Lord, and His statutes, which I command you this day for your good! (Deuteronomy 10:12–13).

> The Lord is good, a stronghold in the day of trouble; and He knows them that trust in Him. (Nahum 1:7)

> The Lord is righteous in all His ways, and holy in all His works. (Psalm 145:17)

One of the most often-quoted passages of scripture regarding the goodness of God is this:

> I had fainted, unless I had believed to see the goodness of the Lord in the land of the living. (Psalm 27:13)

> Or do you despise the riches of His goodness, forbearance, and longsuffering, not knowing that the goodness of God leads you to repentance? (Romans 2:4)

The goodness of God leads us into the bloodiest contest of love throughout all ages: our sin nature versus His redemptive love.

God's goodness challenges all our struggles, priorities, agendas, designs, plans, dilemmas, and adversities. God's goodness eclipses our selfish desires and calloused hearts.

God's goodness sets our lives apart so that we may be illuminated by His Holy Spirit. His goodness leads us (out of our Adamic position [into repentance]) into a place of justification by our faith in His goodness (grace) toward us:

> By grace you have been saved, through faith—and this is not from yourselves, it is the gift of God [goodness]. (Ephesians 2:8)

The goodness of God sets us apart from the world into which we are sent. We are, by His goodness and grace, "in the world but not of the world" (see 1 John 2:15–17).

Paul is sitting in the flickering candlelight, his inkwell dripping with a commitment to write his final words. He's cold. He's lonely. He's broken. He's scarred, but he's not scared. He writes a word of revelation: "Rejoice in the Lord always, again I say, Rejoice!"

Why? How could Paul write of such love in the midst of so much suffering? Because he had found that, in the goodness of the Lord, there is a place called grace. There is a place called adoption. There is a place called sonship. There is a place called love. And there is a place called relationship.

Warren Wiersbe wrote, "Christian service means invasions, battlegrounds, weapons, and war." It is God's goodness that protects us. We are to wear His goodness as our battle dress. Our garment of praise (of the goodness of our Lord) is used to silence our enemies. We defeat the works of Satan when we fully surrender and completely trust in the goodness of the Lord. When we trust and obey. Trust and obedience are the left and right shoes of our Gospel of peace!

13

The Preservation Of The Inspired Word Of God

Heaven and earth shall pass away, but
My words shall not pass away.
—Matthew 24:35

Is the Bible, which we hold in our hands today, the true Word of God, as God delivered it through the prophets and apostles? How may we know this? Can we really be sure? Centuries before the invention of the printing press, the biblical records were copied by hand. Were any of these sacred writings adulterated by the scribes? Did they add or take away from the Holy Writ? These are all rational questions, and they demand an intelligent and diligent search. Let us pursue this line of inquiry.

The God, who is the writer of the inspired record, was careful through infinite wisdom to preserve the true Word. If an omnipotent God gave us these writings, He is qualified to preserve them since they were given for the redemption of His image creatures.

The first thing we should look at in our quest to answer the questions is textual criticism.

The scientific study of the preservation of the true text of the scriptures is referred to as textual criticism. It is one of the most rewarding fields of study in the theological world. Nothing could be more interesting to any student of the Holy Scriptures.

While there is ample evidence outside of the New Testament, most evidence originates from within the New Testament itself. Because the New Testament was written a long time ago, people ask, "How do we know that what we have today hasn't been changed over the years?"

The answer is: we do know. We know through a science called textual criticism.

One way of looking at textual criticism is to understand that it works like this: The more manuscripts you have, and the earlier they are, the more you can be sure about what the originals said.

The following is a table that illustrates the science of textual criticism:

- The works of Herodotus and Thucydides were written in the fifth century BC, but the earliest copies we have are dated AD 900. That is a span of 1,300 years, and we only have eight copies. Yet no classical scholar doubts their authenticity.
- With Livy's *History of Rome*, we find a nine hundred-year gap between the writing of the text and the earliest known manuscript, and we only have twenty copies.
- With Caesar's *Gallic War*, there is a 950-year gap, and again, we only have nine or ten copies.
- With Tacitus, there is a thousand-year gap and twenty copies.
- The New Testament was written between AD 40 and AD 100, the earliest manuscripts we have are dated AD 130, and there are 5,309 Greek manuscripts, 10,000 Latin

manuscripts, and 9,300 other manuscripts. These numbers are unique among all ancient writings.

F. J. A. Hort, one of the most renowned textual critics who ever lived, said, "In the variety and fullness of the evidence on which it rests, the text of the New Testament stands absolutely and unapproachably alone amongst ancient prose writings."

What is telling is that no secular historian has disagreed with F. J. A. Hort.

The first copy of the New Testament in Greek was published by Erasmus in 1516, and for two hundred years, this edition, called the *Textus Receptus*, reigned supreme. In 1611, the King James Version was authorized and translated from this text. Among scholars, there was an intense desire to locate the oldest possible manuscripts and to obtain those that appeared at the beginning of the Christian era.

Could these writings be found? If so, where were they?

Thus began a long and faithful search.

The original New Testament writings were in rolls sent to the places where they were addressed. As an example, some scholars think that Matthew was written for the Palestinian and Syrian Christians and circulated by the Christians at Antioch. Some think that Mark was written for the churches in Greece and circulated by the churches of Macedonia. It is believed that John was written in Ephesus and circulated particularly in Asia. The New Testament is a compilation of many writings directed to various congregations. At the close of the first century and the beginning of the second, we have all the writings complete.

The Bible is the most vetted document in the history of the world. As we've seen, there is so much historical documentation that exists to confirm the faithful transcription of scripture. In fact, of the more than 5,800 known Greek New Testament manuscripts, there are more than 2.6 million pages! That equates to one mile of New Testament manuscripts (and 2.5 miles for the entire Bible), compared with an average four feet of manuscript by the average classical writer. Combining both the Old and the New Testament, there are more than sixty-six thousand manuscripts and scrolls that speak to the validity of scripture!

Recently, Samantha Carey wrote an article for Digital Fire University in which she unpacks the true desires of millennial Christians:

> The Millennials are not kids anymore. They are graduate students, working professionals, and parents of young families.

She shared a note she'd received from a millennial who had stopped regularly attending religious services in his early adult years:

> What we're looking for in religion is an experience so real, so gripping, it knocks us breathless. We want our lives to be overturned. The world is cruel. We battle with fear and hurt on a daily basis. We tread water, desperate for the answer to life. We want something that will finally give us the answer. We want something we'd suffer torture for. We want something more real than a thesis in our heads.

This is fascinating!

This generation and those who follow want the real thing. They want answers. They want purpose. They want ... Jesus!

They want to know about the Divine guide for their journey into eternity.

14

From Scroll to Leaf: The History of the Book

The change from book roll to codex (i.e., a book with leaves) came about in around AD 300. After the codex came into existence, roll books were often cut up and fastened together at the side so that the reader could turn to passages easily and quickly.

Codices were written in large, even capital letters called uncials. At the beginning of the seventh century, a different kind of Greek manuscript began to appear. It was called minuscule or cursive. It was a running handwritten manuscript and was written in much smaller letters. By the ninth century, no more uncials were employed by scribes. In this great quest, we must find manuscripts written with uncials—large capital letters. This particular kind of writing was present in the earliest Christian writings. Uncial letters were employed in the first manuscripts.

In the past few centuries, Greek scholars have spent their lives seeking out and obtaining these manuscripts. They have paid untold prices and endured much suffering to obtain the original Word of God. Untiring efforts have been made so that this wonderful cause can be brought to the attention of those who are diligent and who want to know the whole truth concerning the Word of God. Thank God for the diligent!

Truth is never an easy taskmaster. We must be real disciples if we are going to discover the rare gems of God's Word. The Lord blessed these scholars in their search for the ancient writings.

One of the most romantic stories you'll ever hear is about the discovery of the "Aleph." The *Aleph* is the alphabetical designation for the *Codex Sinaiticus*, which was discovered by Constantin von Tischendorf in a monastery at the base of Mount Sinai in the desert beyond the Red Sea.

For centuries, this manuscript lay untouched by human hands in an old monastery and was accidentally brought to light by Professor Tischendorf. Tischendorf, a world-leading biblical scholar from Leipzig University, had been traveling throughout the East and searching all libraries for the texts of scriptures. In 1844, he came to the monastery of St. Catherine, located at the foot of Mount Sinai. In the hall of this monastery, there was a basket of parchments used for starting fires. Tischendorf looked at these parchments and recognized them immediately. They were the most ancient manuscripts he had ever seen. Unable to conceal his joy, he aroused the suspicion of the monks, and they refused to let him have the codex, thinking it might be of some value to them of which they were unaware. He persuaded them to let him have forty-three sheets of the codex; they refused to allow him to take any more, although they were destined for the fire.

In 1859, Tischendorf came back with a commission from the Russian emperor to secure the rest of the leaves. This trip was sponsored by the Russian government. The second visit was a complete failure. The codex had disappeared, profoundly disappointing the great scholar.

One evening, while walking in the grounds with a steward of the monastery, he was invited to his room to have some refreshments. While the visit was in progress, this monk produced a bundle wrapped in red cloth. To Tischendorf's utter surprise, he found the bundle that had been in the wastebasket on his first visit, as well as other parts of the Old Testament and the complete New Testament—the only ancient Greek manuscript containing all the New Testament that has ever been found. When this was placed in his hands, he knew immediately that he held the most treasured biblical discovery in existence. It was written in about AD 350, about the time the codex came into existence.

Tischendorf brought the manuscript to the Imperial Library at St. Petersburg and gave it the name *Aleph*, the first letter of the Hebrew alphabet. On December 24, 1933, *Aleph* was purchased by the British government for $500,000 and was placed in the British Museum.

Aleph is by no means the only ancient codex that has been discovered. *Codex A, Alexandrius*, is almost as old and also in the British Museum. It was named after the famous library in Alexandria. This was presented to Charles I in 1628 by Cyril, the patriarch of Constantinople.

Another equally ancient Greek manuscript is *Codex B*, which is called *Codex Vaticanus* because it is in the Vatican Library in Rome. It was written about the same time as *Aleph*.

One more interesting manuscript is *Codex C, or Codex Ephraem*. It was brought from the East to Florence, Italy, in the sixteenth century, and a few years later, it was placed in Paris, where it has remained ever since. This codex is a palimpsest, which means that the parchment was used twice. After it had been studied carefully, experts found that it contained writing over an older script. By careful analysis, it was found that the older writing was in uncial script. Luckily, there are chemicals that, when applied to old manuscripts, help revive their ancient form. Through this process, it was found that the entire New Testament was written on this parchment, and it was brought to light through the use of these chemicals on *Codex C*.

Many years ago, an assembly of scholarly men around a dinner table in England posed this question: If every copy of the present New Testament were destroyed, would it be possible, through the quotations of the church fathers of the second and third centuries, to reprint the New Testament? At that time, no one was able to answer this question.

Two months later, one of the men called upon Sir David Dalrymple, who had also been present at that meeting. Sir David asked his visitor if he remembered the question that had been asked at the meeting. Sir David said to this friend, "Look at these books. I have found all the New Testament through the quotations of the church fathers. I possess all the existing works of the fathers of the second and third centuries. From their writings, I am able to find all the New Testament except eleven verses."

The early church fathers were Polycarp of Smyrna, Papias of Hierapolis, Clement of Rome, Irenaeus of Lyons, Tertullian of Carthage, Clement of Alexandria, and Origen and Eusebius of Caesarea. All of these were great expositors of the written Word of God.

There are many ancient manuscripts of the Bible in Latin, Syrian, Coptic, and other languages. Each of these helps verify the true and exact Word of God. The Word of God is the supreme rule of the Christian! Trust it.

15

Archaeological Evidence That the Bible Is True

Archaeology has produced great evidence of the validity of the scripture through its discoveries.

The ancient cities of Egypt, with their palaces and tombs of the past, hermetically sealed by the drifting sands of the desert, contain wonderful testimony of the Word of God.

The archaeologist's spade has dug deep into the sands, opening the graves of the past and unearthing the streets and thoroughfares of the ancient civilizations. Among these findings, we have records of people's daily lives. Many of these were recorded on papyri, made from the stalk of the papyrus plant, which grows abundantly on the Nile. In many other parts of the world, this same material was used to record the activities of past civilizations; all of these records had long been destroyed, but in Egypt, buried beneath the dry desert sand, they were wonderfully preserved.

After careful examination of the findings by scholars, it was discovered that the Greek in which the New Testament was written was a special kind of language. This Greek was known as Koine

Greek. By unearthing these records of ancient Egypt, they found that this kind of Greek was spoken by the people and was the common, everyday language used at the time of the writing of the New Testament. This explained many other idioms of the Bible. And, searching more diligently, they found that many of the ancient papyrus manuscripts from these lost civilizations contained many parts of the scriptures written in the same form of Greek. This was further confirmation that God had preserved His Book through the ages.

In His wise providence, the Lord allowed many copies of His Word to be transcribed. Archaeology has discovered many of these writings in ancient tombs, on rubbish heaps, in libraries, and in the writings of the church fathers. The large number of manuscripts seems almost incredible. They arise from every part of the ancient world and cover the period of the New Testament—plus the scope of the whole Bible. When all the manuscripts had been studied, checked, compared, combined, and grouped, we had our final answer concerning God's eternal Word.

The manuscripts of the annals of Tacitus and a single manuscript containing Greek anthology, as well as the manuscripts of Sophocles, Thucydides, Euripides, Virgil, and Cicero, are rare; very few copies exist. It appears without doubt that Divine aid went to great lengths to provide us with multiple manuscripts of God's written Word. Contained in these manuscripts is the will of God for humanity's redemption. This should help us to see the inspiration for the sacred Book. If all the other forms of literature of the past are read and believed, why would we not take God's Word—original, true, holy, sure, steadfast—and believe it to be the salvation of our soul?

The Lord has seen to it that His Word has been preserved from the fire, wind, rain, storm, and all other conditions that would have abolished His truth from the face of the Earth, had it been possible:

These things have I spoken unto you, being yet present with you. But the Comforter, which is the Holy Ghost, whom the Father will send in My name, He shall teach you all things and bring all things to your remembrance, whatsoever, I have said unto you. (John 14:25–26)

The Holy Spirit brought to their remembrance the spoken words of Jesus that they might be written down, and the Lord saw to it that they would never be destroyed or mutilated.

John, on the Isle of Patmos, declared in solemn tones these words:

And if any man shall take away from the words of the book of this prophecy, God shall take away his part out of the book of life, and out of the holy city, and from the things which are written in this book. (Revelation 22:19)

If any man shall add unto these things, God shall add unto him the plagues that are written in this book. (Revelation 22:18)

No one will escape the wrath of God who seeks to distort the scriptures. God's anathema is forever placed upon such an individual. Be it far from us not to believe the true Word of God, for therein lies the destiny of humanity—and our eternity.

Archaeological evidence continues to regularly validate the Bible as historically accurate. Furthermore, no archaeological discovery has ever disproven any statement in scripture.

Here is a bit of archaeological trivia. Radar images provide evidence of the accuracy of the early portions of Genesis. Genesis 2:10–14 refers to a river called Pishon that flowed through northern Arabia (in Hebrew, the land of Havilah) and was said to connect the Tigris and Euphrates. No evidence of such a river existed until 1994, when radar images from the Space Shuttle *Endeavour* uncovered evidence of a defunct river that once traversed the region that Genesis 2 specifies for the Pishon. Environmental studies indicate that the river dried up sometime between 3500 and 2000 BC, probably a millennium or more before the time of Moses.

James K. Hoffmeier said, "This discovery provides evidence that Genesis accurately preserves very ancient traditions from far before the time of Moses."

16

Intimacy and Awe Dance Together

Extraordinary worship erupts out of the heart of the person awakened to the truth of God's goodness, God's love, and God's sovereignty. It is in the awakened heart that intimacy and awe join to dance in unity. In fact, it could be said that the tablelands of our hearts become the theatrical stage upon which our praise and our worship come together to play.

You've probably heard it said that we praise God for what He's done—and we worship God for who He is!

In *Music and the Arts in Christian Worship*, Robert Webber said, "Praise is born in faith, is an instrument of war and a method of creating an atmosphere for the presence of the Lord. Worship is born from our relationship with God. We praise Him for what He has done and worship Him for who He is."

Praise is a sacrifice we give in faith.

Through Him then, let us continually offer up a
sacrifice of praise to God, that is, the fruit of lips
that give thanks to His name. (Hebrews 13:15)

Praise is our entrance into God's presence. When we find Him,
we worship.

Let us come before His presence with thanksgiving,
let us shout joyfully to Him with psalms. Oh come,
let us worship and bow down, let us kneel before
the Lord our Maker. (Psalm 95:2, 6)

Webber went on to say, "Praise and worship are likened to rings
that are linked together. They overlap, and yet they each have their
own identity."

Worship is a transformative experience we express daily. Our
lifestyles are the result of our worship (our purpose). When we
live to worship, we're inviting God to sit as the sovereign authority
enthroned over our lives. In so doing, we make each moment a
hallowed and holy moment—by our worship.

Today, we worship and praise God as His "new creation
people." As such, we learn much about unencumbered access to
God's presence from the Tabernacle of David.

Here are a few features of David's Tabernacle that illustrate
God's plan for our relationship—our worship and in our sacrifices
of praise with thanksgiving.

First, in this hour, God intends His people to worship in unity,
as one, even as He is one. Jew and Gentile—bonded and free, rich
and poor—all enjoy the mighty outpouring of God's Spirit and His
blessings of grace when we unite in awe of His glory and in intimate
fellowship with His presence.

Second, the prophetic anointing fills the atmosphere where our
praise and worship unite to bless the Lord with our entire heart.

In David's Tabernacle, the partitions were made up of the people worshipping and dancing before the Lord.

Third, in the intimate fellowship of God's Spirit, we immediately recognize His government. In His presence, we are at once struck with the weight of His government, His rule, and His reign. When we worship and praise God and enthrone Him in our hearts, we're allowing government to be on His shoulders, and then His kingdom authority is released in our midst.

Fourth, worship leads us into intimate intercession. King David installed worship teams (choirs) in rosters that never stopped praising God. Worship continued 24-7 (see Revelation 5). This is the picture David held in his mind when he said, "I looked unto the hill from whence cometh my help, my help comes from the Lord." He was looking up to the hill of the Lord and seeing the constant praise of those twenty-four-hour worshippers. Davidic worship is earmarked by its prophetic anointing.

Fifth, David's Tabernacle was a tent set up in Jerusalem, and all it contained was the ark, representing the presence and glory of God. This was prophetic of Yeshua coming to Earth to "tabernacle" or dwell in the midst of His people. The ultimate fulfillment is intimacy with the Lord in the throne room in heaven. The writer to the Hebrews says that by the blood of Jesus we can all enter into the holy of holies. It is not restricted to the privileged few as it was in the Tabernacle of Moses.

Sixth, there is liberty—where the Spirit of the Lord is. David was a flamboyant worshipper who worshipped with extraordinary zeal. He danced, he sang, and he played his harp before the Lord without fearing anyone. David's liberty is also that of the new creation people—people who worship with a true liberty that is found only in "Spirit and truth."

Seventh, there is a harvest—the end-time harvest. The Tabernacle of David represents the place for all of humanity to come and seek the Lord and find Him.

Eighth, the restoration of Israel will be at the forefront of our purpose. The return of Jesus the Messiah is connected to the restoration of the Jewish people because Jesus is to sit on the throne of David! Gentile believers have a responsibility to pray for, encourage, comfort, and "make jealous" the "natural branches of the olive tree" (Romans 10–11).

Ninth, the restoration of the Tabernacle of David is a preparation for the return of Yeshua. The bride of Christ makes herself ready and prepares the way of the Lord (the bridegroom). His bride will be without spot or wrinkle, hence her holiness is imperative—not of works, lest any should boast, but by faith in God's Word, by the blood of the Lamb, and by the infilling of the Holy Spirit.

All will be made ready for the marriage supper of the Lamb through devoted, consecrated worship.

17

The Savior-Sower
and Our Hearts

It's altogether exciting when we meet Jesus as our Savior, Sower, and Shepherd!

In Luke 8, Jesus tells us that the disposition of our hearts is like one of four kinds of soil the sower of seed encounters. It is our responsibility to plow, till, and furrow—and to prepare the conditions for our hearts to be receptive to God's Word.

I have never met a strong person with an easy past. Faith is tested. Trouble in life is inevitable.

One of the most tragic kinds of soil the sower describes in Luke 8 is the fainthearted—that precious person who responds so enthusiastically to the preached Word, but their excitement and enthusiasm for God and His Word doesn't last. They permit themselves to live a life with so little discipline that they never have any structure. They have no roots. They hear, oh, they hear with enthusiasm, but the enthusiasm doesn't go very deep—and too soon, their excitement for the preached Word wanes.

It's only another fad, and the moment there's trouble, their enthusiasm for God and His Word is gone. (Luke 8:13 MSG)

Jesus, our Savior-Sower, is looking for the good ground in which He can sow—the ground from which He can reap a hundredfold harvest!

Will you be His good ground today?

I challenge you to write down one way you're going to receive His promise and see His harvest in your life.

18

Generosity: The Highest Form of Trust and the Greatest Expression of Worship in Trust

The word "generosity" arouses in us a deep sense of gratitude. Gratitude is the response that arises from the life of a person filled with thanksgiving and praise.

The apostle Paul, when writing to the Corinthians, declares,

> Now He who supplies seed to the sower and bread for food will also supply and increase your store of seed and will enlarge the harvest of your righteousness. You will be enriched in every way so that you can be generous on every occasion, and through us your generosity will result in Thanksgiving to God. (2 Corinthians 9:10–11)

The doctrine of generous living comes from Jesus Himself. When Jesus commissioned His disciples, He said, "Freely they have received, freely give."

There is a metaphor that clearly depicts the power, influence, and favor that generosity exhibits in and through our lives. It is the funnel.

God's blessing has been poured out, and we have become the recipients of all that God has given (by position). He opens the windows of heaven over us, and our spirit of generosity, practiced with joy in obedience, is the funnel through which that blessing is directed to us.

God's generosity is seen in creation as well as in His nature and in His attributes. Everywhere you see God moving, you see God demonstrating His generosity toward us.

Our generosity is also a reflection of our beliefs: that God is good, God is benevolent, and God is love.

Generosity is a reflection of God at work in our lives. In fact, you might have heard someone say, "God is good all the time, and all the time, God is good!" This is a simple, straightforward statement of faith. Regardless of how we are feeling at any given moment, or what conditions and circumstances we face, "God is good."

God is always cheering us, advocating for us, encouraging us, and guiding us because He has our best interests at heart. This is a fundamental truth that every believer must rehearse and continually reinforce.

Living as His "new creation" image-bearers, we are made to be the vibrant people of promise who rule over the attitudes of self-preservation with our uninhibited trust; we can defeat the deceptive works of greed with unselfish worship! We do this through practicing the doctrine of generosity, and in so doing, we are insulated from disappointment and despair.

Too many people attempt to live for God with closed fists, their hands tightly gripping all that they know, which prevents them from taking ownership and receiving the blessings promised. So many people check out God's Gospel of generosity, only to fall on the hard ground of disappointment. People who are disappointed with God are ultimately expressing their belief that they think they've been let down, that God did not answer them, or, worse, that He doesn't care about them or love them.

This disposition of thought must be rebuked; if it is entertained, it will lead the disappointed to bitterness. And this is outside of God's governmental order of blessings. To live with a closed hand and a tight fist is to live with a barrier between you and the blessings bestowed on you. In other words, it chokes off the blessings from flowing into you. I don't want any attitude to keep me from receiving all that God has for me, so I live with two symbolic fixtures in the forefront of my mind: the funnel and the umbrella.

Now, I know that sounds silly and quite simple. However, it is the difference between a "more than you can ask for" reality and an impoverished, imperiled existence. It is a true saying that "a poor man must be willing to live with a mind that is poor."

The apostle James showed us the goodness of God toward us:

> Every good gift and every perfect gift is from above, coming down from the Father of lights, with whom there is no variation or shadow due to change. (James 1:17 ESV)

God doesn't have mood swings!

James is writing to Christians who are experiencing terrible persecution. It's easy to imagine that in the midst of their fiery trials, they might question God's goodness. James doesn't cower because of their circumstances. He boldly steps into their circumstances, sets the record straight, and reminds them of God's character:

> Every good gift and every perfect gift from Above. (James 1:17 ESV)

Everything that is beneficial for us and every gift that is complete and without defect or blemish comes from God, our Father. In fact, God loves to bestow good things on you, His child. He loves to bless His children with the riches of heaven. What are the areas of your life where you can identify God being good to you and giving you His "good" gifts?

There are a few we could think of: good health, family, unfailing friendships, freedom, the smile of a child, the singing of the birds, the crescendo of the surf, the majesty of the mountains, the warmth of a fire on a wintry day.

To experience the extraordinary in this life, there are certain truths that we must believe (and act on by faith) and import into our life by a disciplined practice.

Benjamin Franklin famously said, "If you fail to plan, you are planning to fail."

When we look at creation from a biblical worldview, we see an architect with a Divine design, a blueprint. We see intelligence, order, and design. We immediately see the rhythm of a twenty-four-hour day. We see God creating four distinct seasons. We see laws established to keep everything in place.

> By faith we understand that the worlds were framed by the word of God, so that the things which are seen were not made of things which are visible. (Hebrews 11:33)

Framed means to be framed or created (equipped); to be created, furnished, and prepared for a use or purpose.

The plan of creation was to ultimately make known to us the invisible qualities of God: "through Jesus Christ."

> For by Him all things were created, in heaven and on earth, visible and invisible, whether thrones or dominions or rulers or authorities—all things were

created through Him and for Him. (Colossians
1:16 ESV)

The plan of creation was to make known the glory of God
and the sum of His attributes. John Calvin would say it like this:
"Creation is the 'Theatre of His Glory.'"

During the most challenging of times in our lives, it is our
rehearsal of the doctrine of generosity that reminds us that God
has not changed His mind, His course, or His will. He continues
to work toward our good and His fulfillment.

The redemptive work of God is a story of salvation that is still
unfolding. In Ephesians 3, Paul talks about God's plan being made
known:

> To me, though I am the very least of all the saints,
> this grace was given, to preach to the Gentiles
> the unsearchable riches of Christ, and to bring to
> light for everyone what is the plan of the mystery
> hidden for ages in God, who created all things,
> so that through the church the manifold wisdom
> of God might now be made known to the rulers
> and authorities in the heavenly places. This was
> according to the eternal purpose that He has
> realized in Christ Jesus our Lord. (Ephesians 3:8–11)

In The International Standard Bible Encyclopedia
(revised edition), R. J. Hughes III provides this
insight into generosity: generous as: [Hebrews
nādîb] (Exodus 35:5; Proverbs 19:6); AV WILLING,
"prince"; NEB WISH, "the great"; [hānan] (Psalm
37:21; 112:5); AV "sheweth mercy," "sheweth favour";
NEB also "be gracious"; [Greek agathós] (Matthew
20:15); AV GOOD; [haplōs, haplótēs] (2 Corinthians
9:11, 13; James 1:5); AV BOUNTIFULNESS, "liberal

distribution," LIBERALLY; NEB also "liberal";
[aphelótēs] (Acts 2:46); AV "singleness of heart";
NEB "unaffected joy"; [koinōnikós] (1 Timothy
6:18); AV "willing to communicate"; NEB "ready
to give away."

The person with a "generous heart" (neḏîḇ libbô) of Exodus
35:5 is one who gives willingly, and the Hebrew ḥānan means
especially to deal graciously with the needy but undeserving.
Whereas the New Testament term agathós can be used for any
good characteristic, koinōnikós specifically denotes giving what is
one's own, and aphelótēs, haplōs, and haplótēs emphasize sincerity
in giving.

Generosity is a learned discipline. The apostle Paul, when
writing to the believers in Corinth, said, "See that you excel in this
act of grace" (2 Corinthians 8:7).

In *Act of Grace: The Power of Generosity to Change Your Life, the
Church, and the World,* James Petty says,

> There was a tremendous change in attitudes from
> baby boomers to their children. Boomers wanted to
> be better off than their parents and were generally
> encouraged in that pursuit by their parents. Their
> American Dream began where their parents'
> dreams had left off. It is now a pillar of cultural
> belief that pursuing wealth is something that
> someone should have the unquestioned right to
> do. This belief has affected giving ... Until financial
> security is attained, the prevailing sense among
> young adults today is that any serious investment in
> the Kingdom of God seems premature. Generally,
> it feels to them like poor stewardship to divert
> contributions to a church in view of their long-
> term goal of attaining wealth first and giving later.

Today's millennials are taking another crack at the wealth goal. Yet, in the race to the new dream, there is not a lot of money left at the end of the month—especially if people have used debt to attain a certain lifestyle.

Sadly, the people who have fallen victim to this false belief system are unknowingly robbed of God's economic plan for their lives. To live in pursuit of one's own dreams at the expense of obedience to the law of generosity is to bankrupt the future by spoiling the divine blessings that come from God through His laws of sowing and reaping, firstfruits, and generous grace. God's economy of supernatural blessings goes untapped by those who see the church as a place to consume and not the place God ordained for us to contribute to.

There are people today who claim to be Christian, but they live according to the laws and the economy of this world. As a result, these people live in a constant state of struggle, working feverishly to make ends meet.

Consumer debt is the primary dictator that controls the lives of far too many people. Economic slavery is the result for many who've been seduced into leveraging their futures in hopes of winning the American dream. Easy credit is one of the cruelest taskmasters in our world. In fact, a behind-the-scenes look at the design and purpose of our banking system shows that the will to enslave others has never been eliminated and that slavery has never ceased. The only thing that has changed is the name of what the "debtors" serve and the nature of the razor-wire fence that imprisons us.

The Lord instructed His children in His will and His plan for them:

> And the Lord shall make you the head, and not the tail; and you shall be above only, and you shall not be beneath, if you listen and obey the

commandments of the Lord your God, which I am commanding you this day, to observe carefully. (Deuteronomy 28:13, ASV/AMP)

So many Christians excitedly quote Deuteronomy 28:13, declaring that by some "miracle" God will sweep in and rescue them, promoting them at once from the rear to the front, from the tail to the head of the class.

But this seems a complete misunderstanding of the context of Deuteronomy 28:1–13. It is God's formula, His Divine design for our blessings. It's an irrevocable pattern of promises given with a condition:

> "If you fully obey the Lord your God and carefully keep all His commandments that I give you this day." God says, "If you do those things, I the Lord your God will set you high above all the nations of the earth. You will experience all these blessings if you obey the Lord your God." (Deuteronomy 28:1–2)

The Lord then tells us how He will specifically bless His children's obedience. He speaks with such specificity that the clarity of His promise becomes the charge and pursuit of His people. It serves as their blueprint for a new, non-Egyptian economy.

> Your towns and your fields will be blessed. Your children and your crops will be blessed. The offspring of your herds and flocks will be blessed. Your fruit baskets and breadboards will be blessed. Wherever you go and whatever you do, you will be blessed. The Lord will conquer your enemies when they attack you. They will attack you one direction, but they will be scattered from you in seven! The

Lord will guarantee a blessing on everything you do and He will fill your storehouses with grain. The Lord your God will bless you in the land He is giving you … Then all the nations of the world will see that you are a people claimed by the Lord, and they will stand in awe of you. The Lord will give you prosperity in the land He swore to your ancestors to give you. The Lord will send rain at the proper time from His rich treasury in the heavens and will bless all the work you do. You will lend to many nations, but you will never need to borrow from them. (Deuteronomy 28:3–12)

We are to be the human expression, the image-bearers of our limitless, ever-bountiful, extraordinarily generous God who has given us everything. As God's people, we have this magnificent theology about blessings and money:

God has provided everything for us and He has put all things under our care so that we can both enjoy creation and use resources for God's purposes in His world.

Greg Gibbs, a dear friend and renowned author, wrote in *Creating a Culture of Generosity*:

As His people, we believe that everything is God's, and our role is to spend and invest on His behalf.

As believers, not to practice generosity is to contravene the testimony and witness of Jesus Christ in our lives, thereby invalidating our Christian witness and claims as His followers. Sadly, I believe that one reason so many believers do not know the promise of the blessing that is given to us in God's Gospel through our Lord is because the teachings of Jesus about money, prosperity, and blessings are not being taught in our churches.

The pulpits of America are complicit in the poverty of God's people. Pastors who are fearful to talk about money are robbing people of the brilliant promises fulfilled by God's economy. God reveals it for us to teach it, so that people can hear it, believe it, and be saved by it. The Gospel of Jesus is given to us so that we can be wholly saved: body, soul, and spirit. All of us. That includes our spiritual and physical, our financial and emotional prosperity. We must act on the Word Jesus has given to us with trust and obedience.

If you are a pastor, teacher, or leader of people and would like to learn more about scriptural teachings on generosity and the concepts it employs and the blessings it bequeaths to your people, I highly recommend Greg Gibbs's newest book, *Creating a Culture of Generosity: A Field Guide for Church Leaders*. For me—and the churches I lead—we have found that Greg's *Creating a Culture of Generosity*, along with his consultation and influence, have been one of the greatest investments we have made in the past five years.

If you would like to learn more about Greg and his resources for leaders, go to www.creatingcultureofgenerosity. com or www. gregorygibbs.com.

19

Living Out Our Faith Is Not a Timid Enterprise

In *If,* Mark Batterson recounts a famous line from Benjamin Mee in the 2011 film *We Bought a Zoo*: "Sometimes all it takes is twenty seconds of insane courage."

Vanessa Grzyboski, in an article she wrote for Shippensburg University, said,

> There has been a countless number of times when I have held back on doing something because I felt as if I was too scared to do it. That is the problem in today's society, because I feel as if no one wants to ruin an image that they are perceived to be as. We don't want to partake in something unless we are one hundred percent sure that the outcome will be successful, and we will end up happy.

We live in a state of awkward discretion, striving to find that nebulous space in which we are free enough in our individualistic pursuits to thrive on our personal achievements, but not so different from the crowd that we stand out as uncommon.

The reality is that the future will be given to those who dare to take a stand or step up to stand out. The fear of rejection, the fear of failure, the fear of change, the fear of not pleasing others, and the fear that we'll discover we're not enough are the silent assassins that thrive on our tentativeness and lack of confidence.

We are apprehensive because we don't want to disappoint ourselves. As a result, too often, we bail out on our opportunities before they are able to mature and come to fruition. While we say we want success, we're reluctant to confront our possibilities with the boldness of an adventurer. One reason we do this is because we've never given ourselves permission to "go fail boldly," to embrace the adventure of life with no guarantee of the outcome.

Every person of great achievement is an individual who has experienced some defeat. Napoleon Hill said,

> Before success comes in any man's life, he is sure to meet with much temporary defeat, and, perhaps, some failure. When defeat overtakes a man, the easiest and most logical thing to do is to quit. That is exactly what the majority of men do. More than five hundred of the most successful men this country has ever known told me that their greatest success came just one step beyond the point at which defeat had overtaken them.

There are few examples that are more appropriate for us than that scene of Jonathan and his armor bearer. He was a man whose sense of adventure was only eclipsed by his faith in God, his daring, his love of freedom, and his utter lack of concern about failure. His faith and courage permitted him to adopt the attitude that he had permission to "go fail boldly."

I love the way the Message Version relates this 1 Samuel 14 passage:

Jonathan said to his armor bearer, "Come on now, let's go across to these uncircumcised pagans. Maybe God will work for us. There's no rule that says God can only deliver by using a big army. No one can stop God from saving when he sets his mind to it." His armor bearer said, "Go ahead. Do what you think best. I'm with you all the way." Jonathan said, "Here's what we'll do. We'll cross over the pass and let the men see we're there. If they say, 'Halt! Don't move until we check you out,' we'll stay put and not go up. But if they say, 'Come on up,' we'll go right up—and we'll know God has given them to us. That will be our sign." So they did it, the two of them. They stepped into the open where they could be seen by the Philistine garrison. The Philistines shouted out, "Look at that! The Hebrews are crawling out of their holes!" Then they yelled down to Jonathan and his armor bearer, "Come on up here! We've got a thing or two to show you!" Jonathan shouted to his armor bearer, "Up! Follow me! God has turned them over to Israel!"

Jonathan scrambled up on all fours, his armor bearer right on his heels. When the Philistines came running up to them, he knocked them flat, his armor bearer right behind finishing them off, bashing their heads in with stones. In this first bloody encounter, Jonathan and his armor bearer killed about twenty men. That set off a terrific upheaval in both camp and field, the soldiers in the garrison and the raiding squad badly shaken up, the ground itself shuddering—panic like you've never seen before! (1 Samuel 14:6–15)

Jonathan's heroism is only eclipsed by the reality of his faith and the sheer magnitude of his willingness to face the risks of any failure. Peril pervaded the atmosphere. Danger lurked behind the rocky outcroppings of Geba and Seneh.

Everything Jonathan considers, everything he considers attempting, his "logic" and "reason" scream to him, "This is insanity. What you are about to attempt to do is contrary to the laws of war. No military man in their right mind would attempt to undertake such an operation against this garrison of uncircumcised Philistines."

Jonathan bolted forward anyway! He dared his future anyhow! He leveraged his faith in a "peradventure God is with us," never knowing for certain whether God was even in his spur-of-the-moment inspiration.

Jonathan just knew that where God is in promise, He is in defense and support. His character is the holy guardian and His integrity the steward of every jot and tittle. He sees to it that not one word falls to the ground:

> The Lord said to me, "You have seen correctly, for
> I am watching to see that My Word is fulfilled."
> (Jeremiah 1:12)

> Jesus said, "For verily I say unto you, Till heaven
> and earth pass away, not one jot [smallest letter] or
> one tittle [the smallest stroke of a letter] shall pass
> from the Law, until My Word is accomplished."
> (Matthew 5:18)

So, when God's Word is in it, the weakest can storm the strongest citadel of the adversary—and the righteous can prevail over the might of their enemies. When God's Word is in it!

I see something here. Jonathan's heroism is scribed into the eternal record of godly exploits because one man with a helper and one sword said, "I am not sure, but peradventure God is with us!" I'm not certain. I don't know if God is even with us, but if He is, let us go up. "Come on now, let's go across to these uncircumcised pagans. Maybe God will work for us. There's no rule that says God can only deliver by using a big army. No one can stop God from saving when he sets his mind to it."

Apparently, Jonathan's armor bearer exhibited the same kind of far-out faith:

> His armor bearer said, "Go ahead. Do what you
> think best. I'm with you all the way."

In the face of death-defying odds, two men with one sword said, "Let's go risk defeat with insane faith and watch to see: 'Maybe God will work for us.'"

I am reminded of one of our elders at the Church of Champions, years ago, with nothing more than a dream of his future and insane faith in his heart. He started a small company out of his garage. As a career civil servant and law officer, the odds of his success were against him because he could only work on this new adventure in his off hours, which, with small children, were so slim. But he did something that others might have thought absurd. Instead of taking all the money that he had available to start his company, he took half of the money he had in hand, came to church, and made a pledge to God at an altar of worship. He said, "Jesus, if you will bless this company and bless me, your son, I will put You first and pay my tithes and offerings to You first." That may seem like a preposterous idea to some, and to others, it may seem like something that people say all the time. But there are few who follow through on their vows.

This man and his family did. Every time God blessed them, they would bring their tithe and an offering to the Lord's house. Every time. Not sometimes—every time. Each year, through growth challenges, contract negotiations, long hours, and many, many weekends and nights, through building expansions and acquiring multiple service centers, through the daily challenges of the increased responsibility of more employees and a larger workforce, their faith never wavered. Each week, they would bring their worship to the Lord with thanksgiving and praise.

Twenty years later, his company is ranked as the sixth-largest company in his industry in the entire United States of America. Competitors who told him he was out of his mind, that he wouldn't make it, ended up selling out to him for twenty cents on the dollar. He bought them out and shut them down.

Do not let others talk you out of acting in faith. Your twenty seconds of insane faith will be the difference between living life in mediocrity or exceling in uncommon favor and unstoppable blessings:

> But the people that do know their God shall be strong, and do exploits. (Daniel 11:32)

Write down three areas in which you want to exhibit courage and bold faith.

1.

2.

3.

20

Living Out Our Faith with Certain and Sure Hope

One of the reasons we are anchored by our faith is because our faith is the substance of what we hope for and the evidence of that which we have not yet seen:

> Thy Word have I hid in mine heart, that I might not sin against Thee. (Psalm 119:11)

Because the Bible defines God's attributes, nature, and character, we have confident hope in the Word that shares with us His will and purpose for our lives:

> But these are written, that ye might believe that Jesus is the Christ, the Son of God; and that believing ye might have life through His name. (John 20:31)

And this is life eternal, that they might know thee the only true God, and Jesus Christ, whom thou hast sent. (John 17:3)

Jesus saith unto him, I am the way, the truth, and the life: no man cometh unto the Father, but by Me. (John 14:6)

And we know that we are of God, and the whole world lieth in wickedness. And we know that the Son of God is come, and hath given us an understanding, that we may know him that is true, and we are in him that is true, even in his Son Jesus Christ. This is the true God, and eternal life. (1 John 5:19–20)

We have this hope as an anchor for the soul, firm and secure. It enters the inner sanctuary behind the curtain. (Hebrews 6:19)

I love N. T. Wright's Kingdom New Testament Translation Version:

We have this hope as an anchor for our soul, firm, solid, secure, penetrating into the inner place behind the veil (Hebrews 6:19)

The Word of God gives us insight and clarity into the purpose for which God saves by His redemption.

The Old Testament is the account of a nation. The New Testament is an account of humanity. The nation was founded and nurtured by God to produce the people. The nation was Israel. This was the true vine the Lord planted in the earth to produce the kind of fruit He desired.

The primary purposes of God calling out Abraham from idolatry were as follows:

- To prove to the world that there is only one God.
- To prove the blessing of that one nation serving this one true and living God.
- To receive, transmit, and preserve the scriptures.
- To provide posterity through which the redeemer of the world would be born.

This encompasses the great doctrine of election. Election is predicated on Divine choice.

God became man to give us a definite, tangible idea of God. The Old Testament set the stage for this appearance, and the New Testament describes it. Jesus Christ's appearance on the Earth is the central event of all history. There has never been anything before or since that has changed humanity's thinking, planning, philosophy, and domestic approach to life as much as the coming of Jesus Christ to this world.

It came to us with such grandeur that the whole world has been affected by His coming. To the believers, He is the Rose of Sharon; to His skeptics, He is something to write about. His coming has caused more books to be written than any other event that has taken place in the known world. He was, and is, the Divine and unutterable expression of God, placed as the jewel of heaven at the feet of humanity:

> The stone which the builders rejected, the same is become the head of the corner? Whosoever shall fall upon that stone shall be broken; but on whomsoever it shall fall, it will grind him to power. (Luke 20:17–18)

Our response to His coming is the important factor in our lives. It governs whether we will be kicking stars or shoveling dirt.

You're probably thinking, *Man, give it a rest! We know this!*

But it is by the repetition of this truth that we will get it down into our innermost being, down into our spirits until it changes our psyche. If Jesus died to take away the sins of our world—and He did—then there is no salvation outside of Him and there is no defeat in Him. When Jesus died to take away the sins of the world, He was crowned triumphant conqueror because He made our salvation complete. Without Him, there would have been no salvation. He was raised from the dead despite the Roman seal and soldiers, and He came out victorious over death, the grave, and hell. His resurrection made His sacrifice effectual.

This is why He promises eternal life to all of those who believe His Gospel, like His disciples did at the Feast of Pentecost, as we see in Acts 2.

- The whole Bible is built around this axiom of truth. He is Shechinah manifested.
- The Bible is the record of humanity's redemption in all dispensations.
- The Bible defines what God is in nature, character, and attributes.
- The Bible is the written voice of God.

By and through the application of the scriptures, we are saved from our sins, and our physical bodies are to be gloriously redeemed. The Bible declares a spiritual redemption—and a physical one. This present body that we now have will be glorified in God's own time.

Jesus asked the Pharisees if they had not read "that from the beginning God created them male and female." Where would they have read such an account? The Bible! The Bible is God's written account of the creation of humanity in the beginning. Jesus affirms the Genesis record as God's infallible Word. Jesus was God manifested in flesh. He was aware of what He had recorded about this creation (John 1:3).

It's also important to remember that humans are the only creatures who are responsible for their conduct, actions, and behaviors. There is no mutual likeness of God in animals. The animal is not held responsible for its behavior. Jesus Christ came to redeem humans—not animals, birds, and fish. He did not take upon Himself the seed of Abraham; Christ was God's image. When God's image was finally seen by the eyes of human beings, it was fashioned exactly as Adam was fashioned. Christ came as the Son of man and also as the Son of God—God manifested in flesh. When God appeared to humanity, He appeared as a man. Therefore, we see that we, as human beings, bear the image of our Creator.

In the most intelligent beasts on earth, there is no trace of God-consciousness. Only humans have any God-consciousness or religion. Science has done nothing to bridge that gulf. Humanity made in the "image and likeness" of God is chiefly found in his triunity and in his moral nature. "Man is spirit, soul and body" (1 Thessalonians 5:23). The spirit is that part of someone that knows (1 Corinthians 2:11), and that allies us with spiritual creation and gives us God-consciousness. "Soul" implies self-consciousness.

The body, separable from spirit and soul and susceptible to death, is nevertheless an integral part of us, as the resurrection shows (John 5:23–29; 1 Corinthians 15:47–50; Revelation 20:11–13). It is the seat of the senses (how the spirit and soul have world-consciousness) and of the fallen Adamic nature (Romans 7:23–24).

Humans are the only creatures held accountable to God for their conduct. Jesus Christ came to save us—humankind—from our sins. The Bible was written to save us morally, mentally, spiritually, and physically. God expresses His will to humanity in His written Word to give us an approach to God. We are godlike in the sense that our bodies were formed from the ground (Adam meant "red dirt"), and, following that, God breathed into our nostrils and Adam became a living soul.

Adam received something from God that distinguished him from all other creation. He received something from God that no other creature received. Humans are earthly and heavenly in nature. The infinite and the finite were united when this act of creation took place. That which Adam received from God gave us a distinct position in creation. This characteristic of humanity gave us the ability to reach out of ourselves for something stronger, greater, and more powerful than us, and it afforded us this relationship, which no beast was afforded.

Humans have accomplished many achievements on this Earth—and some in space. To show you there is such a vast difference between God's image-bearers (humanity) and all other creation, ask yourself, "What has a monkey ever done in the way of success? What has a horse ever accomplished? Has an animal ever invented anything? Where are the achievements of the animal world? Where and when did any creature invent, accomplish, or achieve any measure of success that places them in the category of humanity?"

The reason we have been able to achieve what we have is our reason, intelligence, introspection, and retrospection, which affords us a different perspective. Humans—you and me—have the ability to observe our behavior of the day and repent, forsake, and improve for our tomorrow. No animal has this power. This ability gives us our godlikeness, God-kinship, and God-consciousness.

21

God's Word Declares Our Salvation

Only in the Word of God is there a remedy: our deliverance from sin. This deliverance is only wrought by one source, and that source is to be tapped into with one element. That element is faith.

In Romans 4:1–8, faith is illustrated, and I find it helpful to read Paul's letter to the Romans regarding Abraham's faith from the Passion Translation:

> Let me use Abraham as an example. It is clear that humanly speaking, he was the founder of Judaism. What was his experience of being made right with God? Was it by his good works of keeping the law? No. For if it was by the things he did, he would have something to boast about, but no one boasts before God. Listen to what the scriptures say: Because Abraham believed God's words, his faith transferred God's righteousness into his account. When people work, they earn wages.

It can't be considered a free gift, because they earned it. But no one earns God's righteousness. It can only be transferred when we no longer rely on our own works, but believe in the one who powerfully declares the ungodly to be righteous. Or "calculated [reckoned] to be righteous" [the Greek word *logizomai* is used eleven times in this chapter. This teaches us that our faith is considered or calculated as righteousness before God] in his eyes. It is faith that transfers God's righteousness into your account!

Paul then writes of David's faith, defining faith for us:

Even King David himself speaks to us regarding the complete wholeness that comes inside a person when God's powerful declaration of righteousness is heard over our life. Apart from our works, God's work is enough. Here's what David says: What happy fulfillment is ahead for those [the Hebrew word for "blessed" or "happy" is asher, which carries the meaning of "a happy progress"] whose rebellion has been forgiven and whose sins are covered by blood. What happy progress comes to them when they hear the Lord speak over them, "I will never hold your sins against you!" [The Greek uses the word *logizomai*, which means to take an inventory and settle accounts.] (Romans 4:5–8)

You ought to shout about that! God has taken inventory of the virtue of Jesus Christ, and through our faith in Him, His perfect righteousness is now deposited in our account. It is settled; we are declared righteous by faith!

Did you get it? We are declared righteous by God through Jesus

Christ. This declaration is not limited to a verbal announcement; it is a legal disposition that has been forever adjudicated by the perfect judge, accepting our substitutionary sacrifice in our stead.

The challenge we face today is that we are witnessing so many people who claim to be followers of Jesus, but they are looking for the assurance of salvation in all the wrong places. Today, some people think their salvation is based on the good things they are doing in Jesus's name. I have had people tell me that they thought they would make it to heaven because they attempted to keep their good works outweighing their sinful actions. If we ever begin to believe that our salvation is a result of our best efforts, our maturity, our spiritual growth, our good works, or our community projects, we are tragically mistaken. While it is true that all these things are good, and can be evidence of our salvation, they do not provide the basis for assuring salvation. Rather, we should find the assurance of our salvation in the objective truth of God's Word. It is the Word and the Spirit that confirm our justification by faith, and it is in the Word that we develop the trust that we are saved based on the promise God has declared, and the corresponding experience that we have had (see the book of Acts).

How can we have assurance of salvation?

> And this is the testimony: God has given us eternal life, and this life is in His Son. He who has the Son has life; he who does not have the Son of God does not have life. I write these things to you who believe in the Name of the Son of God so that you may know that you have eternal life. (1 John 5:11–13)

Who has the Son? Those who have believed in Him (Acts 1:8; Acts 2:1–42) and received His Holy Spirit. If you have Jesus, you have life. Not temporary life, but eternal.

> And if the Spirit of Him who raised Jesus from the dead is living in you, He who raised Christ from the dead will also give life to your mortal bodies because of His Spirit who lives in you. (Romans 8:11 NIV)

Here are a few more scriptures to help you build your faith, reinforce your hope, and construct your trust in God. The continuum is to trust and obey. It's difficult to obey what we do not trust. It's unnatural. God created us for fellowship and community. We are more ourselves in an arena of trust than at any other time. When you trust, you can relax and be yourself.

God wants us to have assurance of our salvation so that we can fully trust in Him and rest in Him. We were never designed to live questioning our salvation and worrying about our existence and death, consumed with anxiety over our future. For this reason, the Bible makes the plan of salvation extremely clear. Believe in Jesus Christ (John 3:16; Acts 2:38; Acts 9; Acts 10; Acts 16:31).

When we follow the pattern of Jesus's teachings, we learn that we must repent, which is a biblical term that simply means to say, "I'm sorry!" I recognize my sins, and I repent (acknowledge and turn away from them), then I say, "Thank you." We begin to thank the Lord for forgiving us of our sins, and as we worship, we obey His next command, which is to be baptized in His saving name: Jesus Christ. As we worship Him and act in obedience to His Word, we say, "Please." We say, "Please come into my life by Your Holy Spirit and be with me forever. Thank you, Lord Jesus!"

22

God's Word Declares Our Destiny

I have been incredibly blessed with a rich heritage of faith and love. My family's ancestry is decorated with larger-than-life characters who have provided our family with a cornucopia of colorful stories: a history checkered with tales of daring feats, extraordinary exploits, hilarious gaffes, and flamboyant misadventures.

My grandfather and father were both remarkable businessmen. My dad is one of the most driven men I know. To this date, while he is in his eighty-third year, he remains active, and his mind is as sharp now as when he was fifty.

My father taught me so many life lessons. His enthusiasm for his craft set him apart from his peers. There are few men in America who could match his wit—and fewer still who could ever match his engineering prowess. To this date, each of you who puts petrol in your automobile is blessed by his competence and technological genius. I've always said that my dad was ahead of his time, but in actuality, he wasn't. He was on time to help shape us and bring us into our time.

Entrepreneurial spirit, discipline, attitude, and daring run deep in my family. Whether it was from a Fifth Avenue mansion or from the Gulf Coast of Texas, the spirit of the frontier adventurer ruled, pioneering new systems of thought, painting with bold strokes the brilliant colors of "Go fail boldly" on the blank canvas of "This has never been done before."

This is one of the distinguishing traits of our family, and it has been one of the defining attitudes of my life. Throughout my life, I have been afforded opportunities to sit at tables with people far more accomplished and much wiser than me. One of the main reasons I've been invited into their worlds of both business and ministry is because of the way I was brought up to think.

My dad has a thousand idioms and ten thousand more cute aphorisms. You never know what is going to come out of his mouth, but if you listen, you'll surely learn something. He has a way with words, and it is in his words that I hear precepts and concepts. His sayings are not a string of hollow notes made from verbs, adjectives, and nouns.

He has a few sayings that he reserves for those special occasions when someone would challenge his set deadline for completion of a project, which, by the way, occurred weekly. When I, or others around him, would dare to make an insinuation that his timeline was not reasonable, nor would it be doable, he lit up as if he were the grandmaster of the new parade in town. He said, "Young man, Rome wasn't built in a day, but a Hutchins didn't have that contract!" While we were sure that he had not considered our need for sleep, he was certain that we would rise to the occasion and meet the challenge. I think he also often forgot that things he could engineer in minutes took other people days and weeks, sometimes a lifetime, to digest and figure out.

My father never—not one day of my life—let me feel or believe that I was designed or destined to be ordinary. He frequently told me, "You are not ordinary!" He taught me that, to speak to your future, you had to see your future, and whatever you spoke was what your heart had already settled on.

My dad frequently reminded my sister and me that "for as a man thinketh in his heart, so is he" (Proverbs 23:7).

When I was a baby, after having been saved by God from dying as an infant, my father tells the story that when I first started talking, he asked me, "Where does an egg come from?" The story goes that I answered, "Eggs come from Henke's." That was it.

My dad left the hustle and bustle of Houston's city center, drove thirty-five miles north, purchased five acres of land, built a home, and erected a barn. My father wanted to make certain that I grew up with a sense of how things really worked: the care and responsibility that comes with living our daily life as stewards of God's blessings, interdependent with all of creation. He wanted his son to grow up knowing where our food originated and how God made the world and all things in it. That's my dad.

In fact, his decision at that moment changed the course of my life. To this day, I have a dream of having a camp where we can bring our young people: those children who grow up in an urban environment, many of whom are living in single-parent households; the children who might otherwise not be able to afford such a life-changing experience. I dream of introducing them to the freedom of wide-open spaces and teaching them about nature, ecology, and wildlife.

For example, I was born and raised in a state that covers 266,807 square miles, or 167.5 million acres, and it is second only to Alaska in land area. As a result, Texas deals with variations of climate and landscape. Our impressive topographic diversity provides us with ten different ecoregions that range from deserts to marshes, from savannahs to high plains. Yet most of our children never learn that Texas has ninety-one mountain peaks that are more than a mile high. While we live in this wonderful world of opportunity, our kids will not realize it if we don't teach them their relationship to the land and their responsibility and care for it. I have a passion to see our children's eyes light up when they are introduced to the magnificent creation that God made for them to work, to play, to grow in, to learn about and, ultimately, to steward.

I know all too well what impact this kind of experience has on a child's life. It thrills me when I have the opportunity to share with others what my father gave me, to see kids who've never experienced a trip out of a big city getting to go out in rugged, natural landscapes and experience nature and habitats, to learn about our resources and to see our ecology. When our kids learn how God made things, how creation works, and why we manage and steward our lives with the discipline of a caretaker, kids get it. They begin to understand things such as harmony in our habitat; they learn how to promote good health physically, biologically, spiritually, and emotionally.

This leads a child to understand the absolutes of truth and helps them learn the "fixed" laws of nature, which are the portrait of a never-failing, always-abounding, ever-generous God. This brings awareness of how God designed us to live in well-being. I'm convinced that when we show our children how to live and work in a God-designed ecosystem, when they learn the majesty and wonder of creation, they will learn to cherish life and value their fellow humans. These lessons reorder our concept of human life and human dignity as a priority of truth—not a relative truth that is subjective according to the conditions or environment. If we want our children to value life and stop the immoral erosion into an abyss of rebellion, strife, hate, and premature death, we must teach our children that they were made in His image and likeness; they were made to kick the stars!

I'm so excited about our Joshua III Foundation because we're determined to help kids who have no chance on their own to cross what seems impassable to them (their Jordan), to rise above and see things from a different perspective, to innovate, to invigorate their imaginations by showing them how to dream big for their future, how to paint the mountains with a broad brush of hope, and how to dance among the stars. To teach them that their new life is not just a theory, but a reality that will overcome every obstacle they will face with the sure and certain hope they have in Christ Jesus!

This is where our theology meets our human condition. This is where we must take off the neckties of "philosophical suppositions" and put on the well-worn "Wranglers of perspective" and put on our feet the "Ropers of the Gospel of Peace." This is where we set the example to our children that we walk by faith, not by sight, and that we walk with our left foot of trust and our right foot of obedience.

Revelation 21:1–8 records the full destiny of humanity. John wrote:

> Then I saw "a new heaven and a new earth," for the first heaven and the first earth had passed away, and there was no longer any sea. I saw the

Holy City, the new Jerusalem, coming down out of heaven from God, prepared as a bride beautifully dressed for her husband.

And I heard a loud voice from the throne saying, "Look! God's dwelling place is now among the people, and he will dwell with them. They will be his people, and God himself will be with them and be their God. He will wipe every tear from their eyes. There will be no more death or mourning or crying or pain, for the old order of things has passed away." He who was seated on the throne said, "I am making everything new!" Then he said, "Write this down, for these words are trustworthy and true." He said to me: "It is done. I am the Alpha and the Omega, the Beginning and the End. To the thirsty I will give water without cost from the spring of the water of life. Those who are victorious will inherit all this, and I will be their God and they will be my children. But the cowardly, the unbelieving, the vile, the murderers, the sexually immoral, those who practice magic arts, the idolaters and all liars—they will be consigned to the fiery lake of burning sulfur. This is the second death.

All that God did was leading to this moment in time. From the creation of Adam until the redemption of Adam, future generations were to come to the great moment in time when we would be safely redeemed and forever safe with the God of his salvation.

We are introduced to the reality that in this "location" of redemptive truth, all people are always safe, secure, delivered, elected, justified, and glorified in the immortal dimension.

They are on the other side of death, grave sin, sorrow, sickness, and any other causes of disappointment in life on Earth. Humanity will have broken into the immortal dimension and come into the full possession of all that God has prepared for us from the foundation of the world. Every dispensation will be consummated in the final act of God and His love for us. We will be eternally redeemed. We will be kicking the stars!

Conclusion

For centuries, Jesus has been building His church with people. These people have individual stories written from the inkwell that flows with the river of His redemptive love!

In *Lessons of the Ages for This Age*, W. A. Mason wrote, "God revealed Himself to man in every age to keep us His testimony on earth."

God has chosen to disclose Himself to us: His creation. That's what revelation means: God unveiling Himself to us.

God reveals Himself to us because He wants to have a fellowship with us. We were created to be in relationship with Him.

So, from the dawn of creation to now, from the earliest accounts of humanity to this morning's break of day, God has been pioneering a "new creation" account written in the margins of our failures, sins, and vices.

Out of the horrors of our separation from God by sin and through the perils of attempting to live without God within us— beyond our faults and failures, our poor decisions, and our best gains—He saw our need and He decided to redeem us.

Kicking the Stars is written for those who desire to embrace an uncertain future with a hope that is mined from the absolutes of God's Word.

Our world is reeling from sin-sickness; it is a world in which moral relativists and secular advocates are teaching from their university lecterns that there is "no universal or absolute set of principles or truth." Liberal ideologues are teaching our children to end any belief in moral absolutes and absolute truth. They are teaching that morality—right and wrong, good and bad choices, right beliefs and wrong ideas—is only a version of their advocate. In other words, "to each their own," and those who follow this maxim also say, "Who are you to judge?" They tout, "When in Rome, do as the Romans do."

Kicking the Stars is a corpus of stories born out of life lessons and experiences that prove the principles and practices of absolute truth, as well as the essential doctrine that establishes God's Word as absolute truth and that this truth is given to us for our purpose.

Our purpose is His Passion! His Passion purchased back our pre-Edenic design, disposition, delegation, and dominion. While it seems to be our nature to easily make room for others' opinions and viewpoints regarding our lives, we must be careful not to allow our dreams to be tethered to their perceptions of our limitations or allow our struggles to define our possibilities.

People who are "kicking the stars" are those people who choose to live in determined faith, always moving toward God's promise given to them through His Word. These people don't run *from* the struggle; they run *to* it, ever ready to "contend for the faith once delivered to the saints."

To forge a future out of "what does not exist" requires us to imagine what must be. Scripture teaches us how to take the principles and practices of truth and make them our intentions of faith until they fabricate the substance of our hope.

This is the crucible in which we learn to kick the stars by embracing an uncertain future with the absolute of our hope.

I close with this prayer for you:

> Now may the God of peace who brought up from
> the dead our Lord Jesus, the Great Shepherd of the

sheep, and ratified an eternal covenant with His blood—may He equip you with all you need for doing His will. May He produce in you through the power of Jesus Christ! (Hebrews 13:20–21)

Bibliography

King, R. (2021). "More Than 110,000 Eating and Drinking Establishments Closed in 2020." Fortune. https://fortune. com/2021/01/26/restaurants-bars-closed-2020-jobs-lost-how-many-have-closed-us-covid-pandemic-stimulus-unemployment.

Sweet, L. (2003). *The Church in Emerging Culture: Five Perspectives*. Grand Rapids, MI: Zondervan.

Carter, C. W. (1966). "The First Epistle of Paul to the Corinthians." In Romans-Philemon, vol. 5, 204–205. Grand Rapids, MI: William B. Eerdmans.

Ritzema, E. (2016). "Truth." In J. D. Barry, D. Bomar, D. R. Brown, R. Klippenstein, D. Mangum, C. Sinclair Wolcott, et al. (eds.), *The Lexham Bible Dictionary*. Bellingham, WA: Lexham Press.

Carey, S. (2021). *Three Things Millennials Are Looking For*. Digital Fire University Press.

Hoffmeier, J. K. (2015). *The Archaeology of the Bible*. Oxford: Lion Books.

Kitchen, K. A. (2006). *On the Reliability of the Old Testament*. Grand Rapids, MI: Eerdmans.

Webber, R. (1994). *Music and the Arts in Christian Worship*, 1st ed., vol. 4, 108–109. Nashville, TN: Star Song.

Petty, J. C. (2019). *Act of Grace: The Power of Generosity to Change Your Life, the Church, and the World*, 222–223. Phillipsburg, NJ: P&R.

Gibbs, G. (2021). *Creating a Culture of Generosity*. Rochester Hills, MI: Harpist Miner.

Batterson, M. *If: Trading Your If Only Regrets for God's What If Possibilities*, 177. Grand Rapids, MI: BakerBooks.

Wright, N. T. (2011). *The Kingdom New Testament: A Contemporary Translation*. Grand Rapids, MI: Zondervan.

Hill, N. (1937). *Think and Grow Rich*, Official Publication of the Napoleon Hill Foundation

Dees, C. (1960). *Christology I*. Houston, TX: Christian World Institute Press.

WCCI (2002). *God Questions?* Got Questions Ministries.

Catmull, E. (2014). *Creativity, Inc*. New York: Random House.

Wright, N. T. (2018). *Paul: A Biography*. San Francisco, CA: HarperCollins.

Crouch, A. (2003). *Life after Postmodernity*. Grand Rapids, MI: Zondervan.

McLaren, B. D. (2008). *The Method, the Message, and the Ongoing Story*. El Cajon, CA: Youth Specialists.

Swindoll, C. (2010). *The Church Awakening*. New York: Faith Works.

Printed in the United States
by Baker & Taylor Publisher Services